Going in the Right Direction the Wrong Way, How to Get Back on Track

Build Confidence, gain Clear Direction and improve your Communication

By David Alan Woodier

Going in the Right Direction the Wrong Way,
How to Get Back on Track:

Build Confidence, gain Clear Direction and improve your Communication

ISBN: 978-1-7349983-0-6

Cover design by David Alan Woodier

Edited by Hilary Jastram

 BOOKMARK

Dedication

I dedicate this book to my incredible wife Erin, who is such a loving partner and supports me in so many ways; I wouldn't know where to begin – your persistence and patience with me and willingness to accept and expect the unexpected in any moment is worthy of a saint.

Thank you for creating a space for me to shine whilst shining so brightly yourself in your dedication to art, nature, and animals as well as to compassion, connection, and creating heartfelt experiences. You illuminate lives wherever you go.

I really did see an angel that morning I awoke to your face at Burning Man.

Free Resources

Go to www.inspirationtosuccess.com to subscribe for free gifts, updates, the latest videos and upcoming workshop dates. You can also learn about coaching with me or choose one of my online courses or products.

BONUS: Check out my book page to see a range of photos and stories in this book.

Table of Contents

Foreword

David first attended to my signature seminar program, The Breakthrough Experience®, in 2010 in Sydney, Australia. In the decade we have known each other since we've had a number of meetings or discussions at some of the other educational programs I have presented in Los Angeles, Sydney, Johannesburg, and Houston, where David has been an avid learner of the principles and methodologies I have presented. I've found him to be a great asset to the learning experience as he is very attentive and contributive in his learning process. He has also assisted me in one of my more advanced courses through searching and finding online content that I desired to present to the class quickly and easily.

I find David's use of his international travel tales in his new book helps illustrate his ideas and adds to the value of the content he shares by creating images for us to remember the ideas by. A range of his ideas align with my beliefs around balance in the universe, which resonated with me, and I also appreciate how he has focused on providing practical, easily implementable steps and tools to people who need help with clarifying their direction so they can move forward.

I believe that David's new book will be a great read for anyone who is looking to kick start their situation with practical tools for self-belief and confidence and ability to connect with strangers as well as it provides an introduction to appreciating the importance of our hierarchy of values, a topic I believe is highly worthy of study.

I am a researcher, international best-selling author, and professional educator, as well as the founder of the Demartini Research and Education Institute. I have been educating for forty-seven years. I feel certain that you will glean many nuggets of insightful wisdom from the pages that follow.

Dr. John Demartini – International best-selling author of *The Values Factor*.

Introduction

I was going to conquer the world,...but was distracted by a small shiny object. That's how life has felt for me for as long as I can remember. I'm a real doer, and when I get my heart set on something, I pull out all the stops to make it happen. From moving across the planet for love to skiing off cliffs in New Zealand, to dancing with the Stars in Sydney; when sparkly objects present themselves, I grab them with both hands and take part. The problem with this behavior is that I have felt pulled in so many directions externally in life from all the exposure I've had to amazing things, and partly internally with all the ideas and projects I think of. In my youth, I didn't really feel pressure from my parents to be or do anything specific. That was great, but it meant I had to choose, and as so many of us know, that can cause frustration and overwhelm. In this book, I'll take you on adventures around the world from right where you sit and also share with you the practical wisdom I feel so grateful to have gathered.

> *"We're drowning in options and starving for direction."*
> *Inspired by John Naisbitt*

From personal experience and what I've noticed over time, I feel that due to the incredible advances in technology and information over the last few decades, the problem many of us experience today is not finding a path to follow in life, it's choosing from all the options and knowing how to create and execute a plan to follow it through. That's certainly been the challenge for me.

As a result, we've become actively and insanely paralyzed in the routines of our lives, doing more of the same thing over and over, yet expecting something to change. The painful truth is that only in hindsight do we realize that for years we've been allowing our greatest resource to slip through our fingers: Time.

But it doesn't have to be that way...

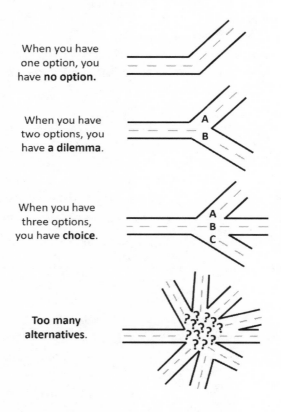

When you have one option, you have **no option.**

When you have two options, you have **a dilemma**.

When you have three options, you have **choice**.

Too many alternatives.

When you have one option, you have no option.

When you have two options, you have a dilemma.

When you have three options, you have choice.

But at some point, too many alternatives confuse us, and we can experience analysis paralysis. Keep in mind that it is natural and normal to want to experience more because it is part of how we grow and learn; it's in our DNA. During times of scarcity and shortage in the last century, many people focused on providing abundance to their families. Today, as a result of conditioning from family, friends, teachers, and modern psychology-based marketing, many of us still live with a sense of lack and a *fear of missing out* (FOMO). We want **MORE**.

But the world is changing because some people have realized they actually want **LESS**. They want:

- Fewer distractions

- Less of a demand on their time

- Fewer choices clouding their judgment and making them feel like they're missing out.

People are looking for help and support in finding their path. They want the skills needed to move in a true direction and confidently communicate to the world who they are and why they're here. If we're honest, they want to be handsomely rewarded for doing this.

I've identified that **Confidence, Clear Direction & Communication** are lighthouses to help us navigate the new world, which is dominated by those who have the **Confidence** to take action. Many people don't realize that healthy confidence has a side effect of helping us move forward. By becoming aware of the risks and benefits of our decisions, we realize that we *can handle the truth* and deal with all that life throws at us — after all, we have survived so far!

Just having confidence, though, is not enough; those who succeed today also have **Clear Direction**. They know where they are and where they're going next. People who move forward are those who realize that...

"You don't need to know the destination to have a Clear Direction."

Having been to, worked, and lived in over thirty countries, including Scotland, France, Barbados, and Morocco, my life path has been anything but clear and pre-determined. I have experienced firsthand the uncertainty of being alone in a foreign country with no money, no job, and no visa to work there, yet over time I thrived. I've gone from earning a pittance picking fruit from before dawn to earning all-expenses-paid six-figure salaries and being flown to work every week. I feel this is in large part due to having the confidence to follow what I felt was a Clear Direction of the next few steps in my life, even if I didn't know the grand plan at the time.

Communication is the final quality that exemplifies those who succeed in this new world. Successful people are aware of how to analyze the communication they receive from the world and do something useful with it. They know how to connect with strangers, navigate conversations, and deal with push back on their ideas.

This new world is one to which I relate and that I've studied for decades.

In my teens, I took many jobs, firstly to make money and secondly to start identifying what I wanted to do with my life; it wasn't that I planned it that way, but in hindsight, I can see that now. The roles were greatly varied: I was a morning newspaper delivery boy in England and would wear only one roller-skate so I could climb the stairs in the apartments, I sold fruit and vegetables out of a truck in the Swiss countryside during my summer holidays with my mother's relatives who lived there, I packed bacon and netted joints of pork at a local butcher, I served in the Battle Axes gastro pub north of London, and moved all kinds of goods around Switzerland, helping out my relatives on an 18-wheel articulated vehicle.

Later, I tried many other jobs and was a chef and temporary manager of a 13th-century hotel near Cambridge, a barman in Hong Kong, an exchange coordinator in France, and a French teacher for children. From Australia to Vietnam, I was a research assistant, a graphic designer, project administrator, management consultant, corporate trainer, and an executive director. Not to mention trying my hand at network marketing, life coaching, and running my own business.

The purpose of all this work experience was to discover my path and what I was supposed to do in life. But I didn't find the answer...

So, I started my *further,* further education. I studied modern psychology, philosophy, all about health, current affairs, sales, love languages, and how to teach. I followed my gurus from London to Sydney, Houston, to Hawaii. I fire-walked, snapped arrows with my neck, hypnotized people, silently meditated for ten days straight, and fasted on water alone for twenty-one days.

All this experience has cost a fortune financially—over $120,000 in tuition and expenses for my studies. Whilst studying, I distanced myself from my family and friends. I never put down roots and, even today, don't have a town I call home.

However, it has all been worth it as I feel strongly connected with who I am, which gives me access to peace in any moment.

I feel confident in life and that I have a solid knowledge of the world, yet I am still humble to the universe's magnitude and wisdom. The experiences I've had and the people and animals I've met have truly been blessings in my life, and much of that is thanks to the investment I made in myself over all those years.

I've learned how to play the game of life and succeed: I've learned how to make money and enjoy it, as well as deal emotionally with being penniless. I've learned how to accept myself and others for who they are. I've also learned how to love and appreciate all the challenges and surprises that life has offered — both good and bad — and I've learned how to live a fulfilled life.

> *"Why go to the starting line when you can*
> *go straight to the finish?"*
> *Huggy Bear*

The fantastic news is that you don't need to do everything I did to get the knowledge. You don't need to spend two decades studying and invest $120,000 of your cash. One of my highest values is teaching, so I consistently look for ways to share my gems of wisdom in an easy and practical way for you.

By simply following a few guidelines from the pages in this book, the three-degree change you make in your life now will result in a completely different future. You will learn how to take action toward what is important to you and enjoy the process.

I will help you build your action-taking muscles without you even realizing it, so you get to enjoy more of what life has to offer and let go of what holds you back.

I will help you see the direction in which you want to be going, so your internal Google Map directs you along that path without you even thinking about it.

I honestly believe that when you implement even a portion of the ideas I share, you will become more certain of your direction, and more self-confident and attractive to others. You will also become an incredible role model for those you inspire.

> *"Shine your light so brightly*
> *it illuminates the path for others."*

I'll be explaining what Internal and External Confidence are and how to instantly increase their effectiveness for you so you can act and gain acceptance of others.

You'll learn how to communicate more effectively than ever before with specific phrases to use when you get tongue-tied, which will guide people to help you in your vision. These improved communication skills will also help you become healthier, better equipped to connect to the world, and wiser in your decisions.

It's time to turn the page and start the adventure you have been waiting for...

Chapter 1:
It's Life, but Not as We Know It

People are acquiring fame and success today in the most unlikely places and at an exceedingly rapid pace, such as Wim Hof who is a Dutchman known for his ability to withstand icy cold temperatures for long periods and he makes a living teaching others to hike icy mountains in winter or singer Carly Rae Jepsen who shot to worldwide stardom after Justin Bieber tweeted a single video of her performing one of her hit singles, "Call Me Baby." There are now more opportunities to learn and a greater array of resources allowing us to succeed against the odds.

Success is not limited to financial success, either. Some people value family and create the most exquisite environments for their loved ones. Some dedicate themselves to faith or an occupation, whilst others focus on their bodies and minds. More people than ever before are achieving fulfillment by focusing their time and energy on the things they value most.

Our achievement is only limited by our effort and ability to find strategies that work for us in an attractive way. When we find something attractive, it draws our attention and focus. If our strategies for success work for us and also draw our attention, we are likely to continue to use them, and this is what I intend to share. I provide some ideas and insights, but also specific steps and strategies to make things fun and easy. Many of us know what to do but aren't necessarily doing what we know, and I want to share what I've learned that can help you move to a place of deliberate action. When people are successful in their field, it is not in spite of life, but *because* of life. Many stories of great individuals show time and again how their initial handicap became an attribute like the tiny and kinda funny-looking Dany DeVito who became a well-known movie star or John Demartini who was dyslexic, dropped out of school in his early teens to hitchhike to Hawaii from Texas and became (IMHO) one of the greatest philosophers we've ever had.

Things Have Changed...

Before computers were commonplace, there was a belief they would revolutionize the world and take away the jobs we didn't want to do. This would create more free time for us to pursue our hobbies and dreams.

In today's world, there's more going on than ever before, in all parts of our lives, at all times of the day, across all our senses, in the air, land, sea, every corner of the globe, and even space.

Mobile phones alone have provided a pocket computer so small and so powerful it allows us to stay connected to the world almost no matter where we are.[1]

Air travel is also an incredible tool compared to the past. Not only is it accessible to the masses from a price perspective (remember, it used to be that only rich people had the funds to travel this way), but it is also much faster, safer, and way more comfortable.

Manufacturing technology now allows us to produce bigger, better, faster, stronger, cheaper, and more diverse products to cater to all our desires...and if the item you want doesn't yet exist, we can now 3D print it out of plastic, metal and combined materials. Recent advances in this area have even

---

[1] *A phone today contains more technology than the first spacecraft to leave Earth and easily more than the whole planet 100 years ago.*

led to the ability to 3D bioprint[2], which is used to create human-like tissues and organs for testing drugs!

In the entertainment industry, we can now film, edit, produce and sell a motion picture using a single laptop whilst sitting by a pool. (Quite appropriately, as I write this, I am in fact sitting on a pool lounger in a hotel in Santa Monica). Holograms[3] are used at concerts to allow dead musicians to perform with live ones in what appears to be real-time. We truly live in an amazing era.

With all the changes, new occupations have evolved and added to the variety which previously existed. In addition to the more standard roles such as accountant, teacher, or chef, you can now create a vocation doing almost anything. Some of the more unusual roles I've heard about include tree surgeon, professional cuddler, and specialist kidnapper. (Yes, you can pay someone to kidnap and torture you for the experience!) There are more ways to make money today than ever before in the history of humans.

However, the abundance of opportunity has also birthed a level of overwhelm we've never before experienced. With so many choices and demands on our attention and time, people feel constantly stressed or pressured. Overwhelm can lead to depression and, at an extreme level, suicide. During my lifetime alone, the suicide rate worldwide has increased by sixty percent[4]. South Korea, the home of Samsung, has the highest figure for a developed country. There are actual teams

---

[2] *https://en.wikipedia.org/wiki/3D_bioprinting*
[3] *Here's an example from ten years ago!*
https://www.youtube.com/watch?v=Cqfa-u3DSdk
[4] *According to http://www.worldatlas.com*

of people whose job it is to monitor the city bridges[5] and intervene when they see someone considering jumping.

Another concern is that people are losing themselves in this world of opportunity. Instead of using technology to improve their lives, they are using it to escape and distract themselves from achieving fulfillment and sharing their gifts. They are spending ever-increasing amounts of time staring at videos and scrolling through their friend and image feeds, binge-watching TV series, and bouncing around the internet, distracting themselves with shiny objects. I know. I've done this for years.

What most of us would really like is a break. A break from the noise. A break from the notifications. A break from the tasks. A break from the temptation. A break from the abundant monotony of just trying to stay above water with all the demands on us and our time.

We need a new approach as, clearly, things aren't working the way they are. We have to find a way to balance all the opportunities and demands in the modern world.

"NO is not a 4-letter word."

But we have to start saying no. If some people can't do this, they will literally be driven to suicide — as the percentage reflects. They will decide to check out because of the expectations put upon them by family, education, societal conditioning, and the often unachievably high and unrealistic expectations they demand of themselves. If those people

---

[5] *This video shows the problems in South Korea*
https://www.youtube.com/watch?v=5jYBWBlEd0U

knew how to honestly ask for help, they would often be rewarded with caring, compassion, and support.

And then there are the zombies, those amongst us who have died on the inside and are just going through the motions, living in quiet desperation as they decide to accept their lot in life and keep their heads down so as not to disturb the status quo or rock the boat.

BUT there will be winners, and if you're reading this, there's a high probability that you're one of them. Winners are people who know how to ask good questions and seek out answers. They are willing to take steps to grow and learn how to enjoy life and contribute more, and they get rewarded for it. If you spoke to most of my friends or colleagues, you'd hear them exclaim that I seem to have so much energy for life and am always positive — well that's not quite true, I'm not *always* positive; however, I'd say I spend ninety percent or more of my time feeling good about life, who I've become and what I'm doing while feeling healthy. This is winning to me. Remember, the quality of your life is determined by the quality of your questions, and successful people learn how to ask great questions. They know how to plan their time and determine how their energy is spent. They are the ones who are ready to raise their hand and ask a question or take the first step of a long journey.

Chapter 2:
There Have Been Ups and Downs

I've experienced a lot in my lifetime, and the diversity and opportunities have provided me with some powerful insights I want to share.

I embarked on my incredible life adventure from a tiny island in the South China Sea. Born of a Chinese father and Swiss & Scottish mother, I was literally *Made in Hong Kong* in the 1970s, where I spent my first decade. My father was a chartered accountant who studied in Scotland before we moved back to Hong Kong, which was at that time, a British colony. As a result, he was considered an ex-pat from the UK, so we received a range of perks such as accommodation and annual return travel, which freed up time and money for fun holidays in the Far East. We then moved to the Isle of Arran in Scotland and lived in the house across the road from my grandmother. She actually married the owner of the house we bought, so he just moved in with her and sold us his house! From where we lived you could look out past the pier, along the bay to the village and then if your eyes continued, you'd see a solid forest, with a castle poking its head out and then further back to the glen and then up to the pinnacle of a picture-perfect (often) snow-capped mountain, Goat Fell. After a year in Scotland, my parents found a home for us just north of London, and that's where my formative education took place. In some ways, it was great to be exposed to such different cultures and locations, but it did mean I missed out on building deep, lasting relationships with friends.

When I went to university in Birmingham, I chose a degree in International Business and French because I felt that those subjects would give me the opportunity to work in many different arenas. I'm sure the fact my parents had an interest in those areas also affected my choice. The gamble paid off, and shortly after graduating, I took the first of many contract roles working on a project a long way from home for a management consultancy. I spent hours every week traveling and living in unfamiliar towns and cities, distanced from my family and the people for whom I cared. It was lonely not having friends around, and at times, I really wanted to catch up with a friendly face and have a good connection, but my lifestyle just didn't provide for that luxury.

In addition to being alone a lot of the time, I also carried two other handicaps into my working career. Four years studying had taken their toll on my bank account, and I had considerable debt. I also damaged my back in a roller-skating incident at university, and an overextended back twist, lasting less than a second, had repercussions that left me in daily pain for thirteen years.

Each of these three challenges of loneliness, financial debt, and physical pain didn't set me up for a wonderful future; however, I found a way to turn those disadvantages into advantages.

> *"Good timber does not grow with ease. The stronger wind, the stronger trees."*
> *Douglas Malloch*

Upon a friend's recommendation, I picked up a used copy of Tony Robbins's book, *Unlimited Power*. That was the beginning of my moonlighting career as a seminar junkie. My drug of choice was seminars, followed closely by the spoken word, then books.

Through books, I followed the journeys of *The Richest Man in Babylon* and *The Greatest Salesman in the World*. I saw transformation with the *Alchemist* and took a walk through *Sophie's World* whilst getting to grips with *Body Language*; I *Awakened the Giant Within*, which led me to *Conversations with God*. It made me *Blink* when I saw *What the Dog* Saw and this new *Biology of Belief* led me to understand that I was both *David and Goliath*. I have spent many days locked in a book exploring the world in search of answers to the interminable question of why I was here and what I was supposed to do.

I also dedicated time to listening to find solutions. I filled my ears with fatherly wisdom from Wayne Dyer and Uncle Deepak. I jogged with David Deida, Robert Allen, and Jay Abraham and cooked dinner with past masters such as Og Mandino, Ed Foreman, and Zig Ziglar.

When it comes to seminars, I've been to nearly seventy personal development workshops, from time management and treasure mapping to investment strategies in the stock market and real estate. I've followed the learning path of Tony Robbins's Mastery University from London to Australia to Hawaii. I've taken courses in Bali, Birmingham, and Brisbane and become a Certified Trainer of Neuro-Linguistic Programming (NLP)[6] and Hypnosis. I've done New York Stand Up Comedy and Improv in Hollywood as well as Bootcamps for Brains with Don Tolman to learn all about health. I've spent hundreds of hours studying some of the greatest philosophers at the Prophecy and Empyreance seminar with Dr. John Demartini in LA, Sydney, and Houston.

In addition, I sat in the same place for twenty-eight hours next to a beautiful stream in a rainforest ravine in Australia to learn

---

[6] *NLP is sometimes referred to as modern psychology*

about nature, stayed awake for forty-four hours to learn about my energy and bungee jumped naked to overcome fear. I visited a real-life shaman in Thailand, and I've explored thirty-three countries and moved to both English and non-English speaking nations where I didn't always initially have the right to stay and work.

In short, I've spent forty years learning and exploring the world to find the answers I was looking for to the questions: *Why am I here? What am I supposed to be doing, and how do I do it?* I have more clarity and understanding around this topic than ever before, which I love sharing with others, so I've distilled it down to a bite-sized model for all. But remember, one of the reasons I know this works is because I've tried, failed, tried again, sometimes failed again, and then adapted my methods until I found a way or made a way to succeed. I'd love to share with you how to do that.

There Have Been Challenges Along the Way

I know we are not all the same, and I appreciate that my journey may look easy to some because of who I have become. However, I believe the universe gives us challenges based on a sliding scale. What I mean by that is that life gives you challenges which it believes you can overcome when you're ready for them. I tend to deal with my challenges quietly, but so you understand, there have been some very hard times.

At age twenty-two, I had just finished university and had been suffering a bulging disc in my back for two years. I had $46,000 debt and was about to embark on an adventure I didn't realize I'd been preparing for my whole life.

A 13-year Affair with Back Pain

During my second year at Aston University, I lived in a shared house away from campus. One day whilst racing on a street with my friend, Hussene, on roller-skates, I twisted and stumbled awkwardly. That was the birthplace of lower back and sciatic pain, which radiated down my leg and lasted for over a decade. For the first six weeks after the incident, I walked around like an old man, unable to straighten my back. I had a wonderful girlfriend at the time, Sophie, and when I stayed at her university accommodation, she would sleep on the floor so I could have the bed to myself. After the first few months, I appeared to be on the mend, but the pain and stiffness never completely went away. It stayed with me to the point where I would hold back on physical activities, avoid walking, and constantly be on the lookout for places to sit or stretch when out and about. One time I walked around a festival holding a large bag of ice on my back just so I could keep going through the pain.

As a man, I felt particularly vulnerable at the thought of having to protect a loved one in a physical situation. With the sometimes-debilitating back pain I suffered, it meant I didn't feel anywhere near as strong and confident as I wanted.

So, to solve my problem, I tried osteopaths, physiotherapists, and massage. I went to Reiki masters and had Bowen therapy. I tried acupuncture, cupping, Chinese herbs, and other plant medicine. I even frequented a therapist who used an old torture method where I was strapped face down on a split bed which folded at my hips to stretch my body. Some of these techniques did help improve the situation. However, it wasn't until I dedicated time and energy to a consistent course of regular chiropractic care that I remedied the situation. Now I no longer have back pain, but I do stay active to keep it that way.

Self-belief was another ingredient that led to that moment thirteen years later when I realized the pain had gone: I was *absolutely certain* I'd find a way to get rid of that pain. I am also sure that my self-belief played a huge role in giving me the life I have today, where I no longer suffer. Without that belief, I would have given up trying years before.

Dear bank, I'm going to Australia.
P.S. I haven't forgotten I owe you $50,000.

My parents have always been good savers and tried to instill that skill in my brother and me. Nevertheless, I still managed to create nearly US$50,000 in debt by the time I left university. I was optimistically sure it would only take me a year or two to pay it all off; I'd have a successful career and be saving thousands of dollars per month. But that wasn't the case. The debts continued to grow. After working in the UK for a year, I decided to move to Australia and New Zealand. I ended up staying there for two and a half years and had a great time, but my debts continued to rise. When I returned to the UK, I found a job promoting Tony Robbins across Europe, which exposed me to more new ideas; however, I wasn't satisfied, and I knew things had to change.

Picture the scene. It was a wet winter evening in a dubious part of Manchester, and the view out my rented third-floor studio apartment window was gray and foggy. The room was cold, and the tinkle of raindrops falling from the ceiling was disturbingly close as they landed in the cooking pots peppered around the room. The warmth and glow of a small two-bar heater gave a little solace in the gloom, yet I was crying my eyes out. I mean, really sobbing, snot dribbling, throat sore, and I felt terrible…in a good way.

I was working through Tony Robbins's Dickens Process, where you internally look at your past, present, and future based on your current behavior, and I was picturing how I would feel about my life years in the future if I didn't change what I was doing now. It was at that moment I made the decision to move to Australia. Despite my debts, the fact I didn't know anyone in Brisbane, my back pain, and the fact I had no visa to work there, I knew I had to leave.

The next day I gave notice at my work, and it wasn't long before I'd bought tickets on my credit cards to fly to Sydney. By the way, I've heard we shouldn't burn our bridges, we should bomb them, which is why I gave notice, knowing that would make me leave. I packed up my belongings, gave my car away, and within two months, I was winging my way Down Under.

When I first arrived in Australia, I drove to Brisbane because it was the biggest city in my favorite climate in my favorite country. Initially, I lived in a VW Kombi camper van, and my full-time occupation was finding a company to sponsor me so I could work and stay. After five months of trying, I eventually found something that lasted about half a year. But for nearly ten years, I lived from visa to visa with the risk of being deported if a job finished, and I didn't have another lined up. I did have to depart Australia twice during that time due to visa restrictions expiring; however, I somehow managed to keep adapting and rolling with the blows.

After five years, I stumbled into a new occupation in training, which really suited my personality, and as a result, I finally paid off nearly $80,000 of debt — the peak of my obligations.

One skill I've been blessed to have grasped over the years is how to enjoy life despite being in debt. I know how much of a handicap debt can feel at times, but by continuing my personal development, learning about myself, being open to trying new things, and appreciating the skills I do have, I've arrived at a place where I make money and don't have debt. I've learned how to enjoy making money, and I've built my confidence to achieve more.

As I mentioned earlier, I've spent a lot of time and energy educating myself about life and trying out the skills I've learned. Although my costs have been in many currencies, I estimate I've invested well over US$100,000 on my personal education and worked for companies across the planet, from massive multinationals to corner stores. I've connected with thousands of people in many walks of life and from many countries — and I've seen that there are patterns.

I've learned how to make money in all kinds of environments, build a career, move bases internationally, and overcome thirteen years of chronic back pain. I've paid off considerable debt, created an incredible relationship and home, built a new life, and followed my dreams. And I believe that I've gone through all I have so I could share some of my learnings with you. Part of my path has been to become a teacher, and I love explaining what I know. You'll discover amazing adventures in this book where you'll find insights you can use to shed light on your own path.

Chapter 3: The 3C Model

There are often two types of education that people need. One is the big picture preparation kind of knowledge to help contextualize and perhaps cultivate new skills — if that's what you feel you need, I suggest reading this book from cover to cover. The other form of learning is Just in Time microlearning information, where you just want to know what to do for a particular issue — similar to what we often do on Google or YouTube. If this is your nature, skip around and try things out along the way, and I recommend marking the book with the points you find important.

I like to use a simple model, which I call the 3Cs because there is a natural upward spiral that we can take advantage of simply by working on any one of the Cs. They are **Confidence, Clear Direction**, and **Communication**, as I mentioned earlier in the book.

The more **Confidence** you have in an area, the more likely you are to know what you want, so you'll have a **Clearer Direction**. The clearer your direction, the more easily you will interact with the world through **Communication**. As you gain experience, your confidence will grow, and you'll be more likely to make better decisions about your next steps...and the process repeats. My model is an upward spiral, which means as you improve in one area, you open up your ability to handle bigger things in other areas. It's awesome!

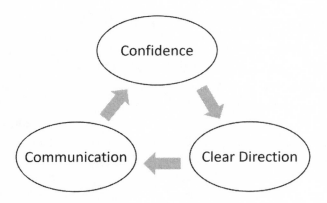

Confidence

Having confidence gives us a feeling of certainty, and action is often a positive side effect of being certain. Being more confident is useful both internally, to help us believe in ourselves so we can move forward with our dreams and desires, and externally, as people around us are influenced by how we appear and behave.

Clear Direction

Having a Clear Direction in life is fundamental to achieving more of what we desire; it also helps minimize aimless activities. Remember, *we don't need to know the destination to have a Clear Direction*. And as I'm sure almost everyone would agree, we are in places in our lives today we could never have anticipated five years ago. The level of thinking that led us to where we were back then is not the same level of thinking we now possess. For this reason, making rigid plans for our lives can be counterproductive. Remember, the samurai sword is razor-sharp and solid yet flexible, allowing it to dance to the conditions around it.

Communication

When we send out and receive communication in a way that makes us feel understood, we feel more effective and appreciated and have more success. It's obvious that if someone speaks a foreign language, the message doesn't make sense, so we take time to translate it so we can be understood. Unfortunately, many people are not aware that even when speaking the same language, we have different ways of communicating. Instead of adapting our style, we repeat what we're saying or turn up the volume and expect different results. Learning how to open, maintain, and close connections with people and deal with resistance can provide certainty and strength in your conversations.

But I Can't Do It

Having a map doesn't mean you will always reach your destination. Likewise, simply knowing about the 3C model isn't enough to improve your life — you have to act on it. But...

David, I don't have the time...

Most people say they don't have time, and with all the demands on us, that makes sense. What I find, though, is that they mean, "I don't think that will be worth my time." Remember, we're all given twenty-four hours of the raw material of life every morning. We can use it, waste it, ignore it or not even acknowledge it, but we cannot save it, overspend it, or draw on it in the future.

People just like you once said they didn't have the time either, but somehow, they managed to learn or improve. You know people like this, and they are now the ones reaping the rewards in their health, wealth, and relationships. It's only with

20:20 hindsight that we realize the effort put in to learn or do something different provides us with massive rewards. The contents of this book are no different. If you like my style and stories, give yourself the gift of at least eighteen minutes per day to continue reading, and in no time, you'll have achieved a result: finishing the book!

I'm different; this won't work for me...

We're all special and different, and some of you may think the strategies and ideas in this book won't work for you. You could be partly right. Some parts of what I share will push you outside your comfort zone, and if you're not ready to go there yet, that's fine. On the flip side, there will be ideas you *are* comfortable enough to practice, so focus on building your skills there. Using one tool effectively can have huge impacts in your life. Each time you improve a part of yourself, you make a quantum leap in what you are able to achieve. It's like when you get to the top of a mountain, and you can see the path ahead so much more clearly. To reiterate: when you improve in one area, you open up your ability to handle bigger things in other areas.

I don't have the money...

Many of the ideas I share with you will have either low or no financial cost. The cost to you is going to be your time, focus, and energy. There may be times that I suggest courses or coaching to further your studies and, yes, that could cost you financially. You'll have to make decisions then as to whether that's right for you. In my opinion, there's a place for cheap, and three areas in which I would discourage searching for cut-price deals are in advice about life, cars and toilet paper —each can result in disaster!

I won't be able to stay focused...

Ahh, the bane of our existence. We believe we have the ability but get distracted by shiny objects and lose focus. The distractions can be in the form of entertainment, social media, exercise, cooking, shopping, tidying, or any other activity to which we turn when we don't want to do something.

The funny thing is that we're all actually fantastic at focusing, but don't always prioritize what we focus on. We're all governed by a hierarchy of values and are constantly doing things to fulfill the highest ones. When we can't see a good connection between what we're doing and our highest values, we tend to look for immediate gratification — and we're GREAT at focusing on that. See, you have the skill already, it's just undirected.

I have explained these potential stumbling blocks to help you realize that you're not alone. We all have challenges and beliefs which are designed to guide us. All I ask is that you remember that you do have a choice. As Tony Robbins says:

"Your past doesn't equal your future unless you live there."

I love stories and sharing useful, valuable tips, and new perspectives. Throughout this book, I'll show you how I've used these skills in my life, so you'll know they work. As you read, you will start to realize your strengths, and with the skills of an aikido martial artist, I'll help you align and redirect them in a more powerful way. As a result, your focus will grow, and you'll be even more successful in what you decide to turn your energies toward.

Chapter 4: Confidence

In this chapter, I'll explain what confidence is, how to recognize it, and how to develop it in yourself. We'll be looking at how our Conditioning, Comfort Zones, and Self-Belief affect our ability to achieve and how we can use our Appearance and skills of Interaction to connect more easily. Don't miss the story about how too much confidence can be a drawback...it nearly cost me my right arm!

When you have confidence in something, it gives you a level of certainty about it. That certainty provides security and stability, which, in turn, permits you to function more fully and comfortably. For example, when you have confidence in a vehicle, you trust it will perform in the way you expect, so as you drive, you're not focusing on the brakes, whether the wheels will stay on or if the engine will fall out. As a result, you can drive with certainty and comfort, and your mind is available to focus your energy elsewhere.

Confidence = experience x belief

Self-confidence is the feeling that you trust yourself and are willing to take action toward what's important to you. You are able and more likely to succeed in your endeavors and also feel that you can deal with any consequences of your actions. Building your confidence to an appropriate level contributes significantly to leading a fulfilled and fruitful life.

> **Confidence is:**
>
> The state of *feeling certain about the truth of something or a strong feeling of trust.* The etymology of the word derives from confidere in Latin, meaning to have full trust[7].

Confidence Is Something You Develop

Many people live with a fantasy that they can and should automatically be far more confident than they are (in all areas of life!) without any specific action on their part. This can cause frustration, disappointment, and depression. Nobody is born with the level of confidence they currently have; it is a skill cultivated over time through experience and knowledge. We would never expect someone to sit at a piano for the first time and instantly be an expert, but we often apply that kind of logic to ourselves. This is particularly true in relationships, where many of us have had no formal training in how to meet people or nurture a connection, yet we're upset when we fail yet again to successfully do so. Learning about and practicing in any area inherently forces you to become more confident. Experience leads to confidence.

Confidence is a journey and a destination.

Despite Hong Kong being an unusual location in which to grow up, my parents and upbringing provided a safe environment to experience life and build my confidence faster than the norm. Living in a foreign country where the culture was very different, and the first language was not English meant that I had to get comfortable not understanding what people were saying. I was also exposed to people of many ages, origins, and values, and this helped me formulate opinions about humans.

---

[7] *https://www.lexico.com/en/definition/confidence*

I quickly learned that although we are all different, 99.9 percent of us are similar, not scary, and are just trying to do our best with what we have available.

Many of us would like to be more confident yet haven't considered clearly what that means or how to get there. As a result, it is difficult to see when or whether we're progressing or what we even need to do to progress.

"Not knowing where you're going is like trying to come back from somewhere you've never been."

We Don't Lose Weight by Staring at the Scale

Many people put the cart before the horse when it comes to building confidence. In a world where yesterday is too late, people tend to focus on the outcome of feeling more confident instead of the activities which result in us becoming more confident. From the valuable 4DX model of Franklin Covey, these are referred to as *Lead* and *Lag*[8] measures, where a *Lead* measure relates to the activities you do to result in the *Lag* measure, which is changing. For example, if you keep putting money in the bank (Lead), you will end up with more savings (Lag).

Despite the Law of Attraction, we know that to build a muscle, we don't stare at it; urging a muscle with positive thoughts to be more developed isn't going to work. Exercise results in a more developed muscle. The same can be said for building confidence.

---

[8] *https://www.franklincovey.com/the-4-disciplines/discipline-2-act.html*

"Confidence comes from experience, and experience comes from doing things when you're not yet fully confident."

What does a lack of Confidence look like?

At a high level, when someone has low confidence in an area, they tend to do some of the following:

- Have doubt in their actions and seem uneasy. This could be noticeable, for example, if someone were giving a speech on a topic they didn't know well.

- Behave without purpose or direction. In areas where we are not confident, we tend to distract ourselves or avoid taking action because we're not sure what to do next or are scared of taking action.

- Think things will go wrong, and they'll not be able to deal with the consequences. Part of confidence is knowing you can deal with the consequences of what happens, and less confident people tend to worry about things where they don't feel confident. *Worrying is negative goal setting,* so it's particularly important to build your confidence so you don't use time focusing on what you don't want to happen!

- Think they're incapable. Not only do we worry about things going wrong more frequently when we're not confident in an area, we often don't feel we can deal with it if things go wrong in an amplified way due to our lack of confidence.

Most of us would rather avoid these kinds of feelings, and having more confidence does just that.

What does Confidence look like?

People who behave with healthy confidence in their lives energetically and literally appear very different. In areas of confidence, they tend to:

- Live with certainty and are more reliable.

- Appear to be on purpose and living with direction and sense of knowing.

- Believe things will work out, and if they don't, they will be able to deal with the consequences.

- Believe they are capable.

Our destination, when building confidence, is to get to a place where we have certainty, trust, live with purpose, believe things will work out and that we can deal with any consequences that come up.

Internal vs. External Confidence

Imagine a confident person — how do you know they are confident?

It's not usually a single thing they say or do to make them appear this way; it's usually a collection of qualities. Perhaps they are very friendly and can talk to anyone, they hold their head high or move gracefully. Or maybe they speak a foreign language, have an artistic talent, and are adept at playing an instrument or singing. Confidence is a word encompassing a range of attributes, and by knowing what the building blocks are to confidence, you give yourself a great opportunity to improve.

In life, we feel an energetic attraction toward people who carry an aura of confidence. This feeling transcends age, origins, sex, and even species. When we behave with purpose, others perceive we are showing that we believe in ourselves and that we stand for a cause; there's something inexplicably reassuring about that.

When you understand what confidence is and take small steps toward building it, you can get relief from a lot of unnecessary stress in your life. You'll be able to take action in many areas affecting your health, wealth, and relationships to become stronger, more satisfied, and wealthier than before.

As discussed, Internal Confidence is made up of a combination of three important attributes: **Conditioning**, **Comfort Zones**, and **Self-belief**. Sometimes our internal belief as to whether we can achieve success is not strong enough when we try to set goals, and we make them too big for our skill level. Setting huge or inappropriate goals when we're not yet able to achieve them can be like trying to ski down a black run on your first attempt. This behavior can even have a detrimental effect because we end up strengthening our failure muscle and thus get better at failing. When you bring awareness to your ability and set goals more aligned with who you are, you have a far greater chance of success.

On the flip side, External Confidence relates to our **External Appearance** and **Ability to Interact** with others.

Internal Confidence

Relates to our trust in ourselves to make the right decisions and behave in a way that reflects who we truly are. It is our ability to identify what is important and take steps to achieve it by hearing or sensing our intuition and acting on it.

- It helps define our path by reminding us of what we love and love to do

- It guides our attention toward what is important

- It supports us in taking consistent action which we don't resent

- It gives us peace of mind and an understanding of life

- It helps us say yes and no at the right times

It reminds us of how successful we already are.

External Confidence

Relates to our ability to attract others and start connections. It reflects our skills at meeting people and showing ourselves in an encouraging light where others feel a connection even at our first meeting.

These topics will introduce you to new ways of understanding yourself and others better, including:

- What makes people attractive?

- What can you do to build your attraction?

- How can you connect more easily with strangers?

- What can you better understand about others, so you're not fearful?

Building your confidence makes you naturally more attractive. Once you're attracting and connecting with people, use your Internal Confidence to build great relationships and wealth in all areas of your life.

In the following sections, we'll cover the attributes of confidence in turn and provide simple suggestions of ways to build those muscles, so you have them when you need them.

Internal Confidence

Do you believe what you are told by the media and in advertising?

When we are conditioned, we react to something based on a stimulus. If we're unconscious in our conditioning, we will see a transformed version of the truth. Conditioning is created by anything we experience in any way. The more emotionally powerful the event, and the greater the repetition, the more likely that the conditioning will create a set of beliefs that will affect your life. With all that's going on in the world, it's important to explore the conditioning you have that is affecting your self-belief.

Nothing is inherently wrong with conditioning (which is simply learning by association), and it is very important in some respects. For example, when driving a car, conditioning ensures we stay on the correct side of the road and keeps us alive!

It is important, however, to reflect on historic associations we've made in our conditioning to see if they are still valid today or if they can be tweaked to better serve us.

I've been lucky to have lived in a range of situations across the planet, and therefore, I have a much higher awareness of conditioning than those who haven't had this kind of experience. My expectations of life have been diverse, ranging from sleeping in wooden shacks on the sides of mountains to being lost in foreign countries with no money to dining with philosophers and training CEOs of multinationals.

The following exercises are designed to help you bring some awareness to your conditioning. You don't need to change anything as a result of it; this is simply about you becoming aware and, if you would like to, you can choose to change.

Un-conditioning Exercise

Answer the following questions to uncover some of your unconscious conditioning. Just let the answers flow. This is only for you, so you can use bullets or any notation which you find easy to understand. If you're doing this on paper, leave half a page between each question. Aim to provide at least three answers to each question. Note: if you read the questions out loud, the exercise will be more powerful.

Un-conditioning Questions A

1. What do I think I should be doing for a living?

2. What do I want to change about my health or body?

3. What should my behavior be like?

4. What should my spiritual practice look like?

5. What am I stopping myself from doing?

Once you have answered the questions above, turn the page.

Good job!

Now let's uncover why you have those beliefs by continuing the exercise.

Usually, people or systems of beliefs have guided you with their philosophies. Their views are guiding your perception of who you are and what a person like you should do.

> **Answer the following question as it pertains to the questions you answered on the previous page:**
>
> 1. Who or what influenced that belief? It could be you or others, someone real, a perception of someone, or even the perception of who you think you are.

- For extra marks, read through your answers, and circle any words or phrases that you feel influence you more strongly.

Then turn the page.

Nice work.

Look at your answers and see if there are any trends.

- Were there certain people who particularly influenced you? Do you need to keep those beliefs? Are they historic or someone else's?

- Did you used to believe something, and without checking, you've kept that view for a long time past its expiry date?

- Are you subconsciously following a path someone else has written for you? Are you sure you want to keep doing that?

- Do you have an imaginary version of you to which you compare yourself and feel dissatisfied because you can't live up to those standards created by you, the media, and well-wishers?

Remember, you can love and care about people, but you don't have to live your life according to their guidelines. You are not them and vice versa, so choose a path and a set of beliefs that closely support you to be the best you can be, as that is what serves us all the most.

Your views may be completely valid. Take a moment to see if they really are. If you have conditioning that is no longer useful, decide to adjust your belief.

Turn the page to learn how to do exactly that.

I have included a re-conditioning exercise to help you find your way back to better conditioning.

It's pretty exciting to know that we are more in control of what we tell ourselves than we believe. I am excited to see how you do!

Just before we finish this exercise, take a moment to ask yourself the following questions, and come up with at least three answers for each. The questions may seem similar to those we covered previously, but they're subtly different. Take note of your responses. These will define a much more aligned version of you.

Un-conditioning Questions B

1. What would I **love** to do for a living?

2. What would I **love** to change about my health or body?

3. What would I **love** my behavior to be like?

4. What would I **love** to follow as a spiritual practice?

5. What would I **love** to do more?

We'll be exploring how you can be rewarded for what you love to do later in the Clear Direction chapter.

Watch out if the word *should* comes up in your answers, look at who is *should-ing* on you and decide if their opinion is valid or even real. If not, perhaps you can let it go because you make the rules in your own life. It is important that when you answer these questions, you feel connected with the response — begin your phrase with, *I would love to...*

Re-condition Yourself Exercise

This conditioning exercise will create different associations in your brain to the same stimulus and is a simple form of self-reconditioning.

TIP: The more emotionally intense you make the reasons in this exercise, the more effective this new conditioning will be.

45

You can do this by completing the following exercise:

1. Decide on a new, more empowering belief to replace the old one. Make sure that new belief serves you, others, and is appropriate.

    - **Old belief**: I should keep quiet in conversations. I don't know much or have anything to say.

    - **New belief**: What I have to say is important, and I'll share it with people who I care about.

    TIP: After you cover the section on values in the Clear Direction chapter, this exercise can be used even more effectively by associating your values to the new belief.

2. Write a list of thirty powerful reasons your new belief serves you and the people around you.

    Reasons (examples)
    - When I share in conversations, I feel more connection.
    - Sometimes, the ideas I share help people.
    - I'll become more confident if I speak up, which will help with other things in my life.
    - Speaking up shows I'm not holding on to an old memory of my ability.

3. Write a list of thirty reasons the old belief is not serving you.
    - When I stay quiet, people don't know how much I know.
    - When I stay quiet, things don't change, and I don't like the way they are right now.
    - When I don't think what I say is important, I'm making myself less than I really am.

- When I don't speak up, people may think I agree with them when I don't.

When your behavior is consistent with your identity, you feel a centered sense of empowerment, and your confidence and self-belief grow. I liken this to a feeling of certainty that things will work out.

How Your Conditioning Can Hold You Back

Conditioning can lead us to hold certain beliefs about our self-worth, abilities, and opportunities. These beliefs prevent us from changing the situation or taking advantage of the possibilities around us. For example, have you unknowingly decided that you can't have the love, wealth, or success you desire? All of us can improve, and my experience in life has been that when we're committed, we can achieve anything.

Amazing Friends of Mine Who Decided to Make Their Own Rules

I know some really great people, and I appreciate their willingness to create their own standards. Here are three of them to inspire you as to what's possible:

Andreas Dagelet, World Hand-Cycling Distance Record, 15,918km circumnavigating Australia[9]

A good friend, Andreas Dagelet, fell out of a tree and broke his back when he was in his late twenties. I met him in a hotel in Hawaii in 2011, where we were both attending a Tony Robbins course, and later, he went on to break the world hand-cycling distance record by circumnavigating

---

[9] _upcs@mac.com_

Australia. Andreas chose not to be conditioned to the idea that a person in a wheelchair is less able than others. He went on to do something 99.999 percent of humans wouldn't or couldn't do. And he did it as a paraplegic.

Hannah Mermaid, Professional Mermaid[10]

Another amazing friend is Hannah. Growing up in Australia, she loved the ocean and felt a calling to spend time in it. She spent so much time there she decided she wanted to be a mermaid. Unlike children who have that fantasy but grow older and let it go, she decided not to accept the conditions of society and carved out a role for herself as a professional mermaid. She is hired for modeling and free diver performances and uses her love of sea life and the sea to raise awareness of ocean ecology and how we can help improve it.

Erin Maxick, Experience Cultivator

Erin is my wife. She is an exceptional person, and since before I met her, she has been making a living, creating unique, heartwarming, and memorable experiences. Working for an avant-garde circus, Lucent Dossier Experience, she has had residencies and performed in iconic Los Angeles locations such as the Edison and Cliftons. Her "job" consists of designing and delivering intimate theatrical experiences such as the Interdimensional Postal Portal (seen on the Orient Express, at Burning Man and private locations around the world) where she delivers lost letters, each a handwritten art piece. On the flip side, she has found work blowing huge bubbles at corporate events and festivals — not something most of us would expect you

---

[10] www.hannahmermaid.com

could make a living from. She has even branched out to working with exotic animals, creating unusual and heartfelt animal therapy experiences for veterans, at-risk youth, and the elderly through her non-profit organization, *The Little Zoo*.[11]

These people did not accept societal norms and conditions. They believed they had something bigger to do, so they took steps toward it. Even though they didn't necessarily know the destination, they knew how to take the steps toward what they most wanted to do. Their Internal Confidence allowed them to see possibility and take action.

I have had some of my greatest successes in life by not abiding by societal conditions and the expectations placed on me. When I tried new things, I found that my comfort zone expanded, and I could achieve more — we'll talk more about that a little later.

Where Are You Charged?

If you touch an exposed wire which has an electric charge, you get a reaction. Similarly, consider the things you react to as the things you are *charged* about. Do you often react to a parent or partner in certain situations? Do you snap at people or overreact if they behave a certain way? Do you wish you were fitter or doing something else with your life, and it frustrates and stresses you, and you possibly constantly berate yourself for these shortcomings? These are all things you have charge on. These things will take up space and time in your mind as

---

[11] www.erinmaxick.com, www.thelittlezoo.org

you think about them, which prevents you from focusing on their resolutions or other, more constructive ideas.

Next Steps

I recommend identifying then reviewing 1-3 areas in your life where you are stressed and have *charge*.

Consider who or what is influencing your beliefs in those areas. It is highly likely you are injecting someone else's values into your world (or, again, comparing yourself to a fantasy version of you that doesn't exist) and then reacting to the expectations you feel you have to live up to.

It is useful to expand your awareness of an issue, so work on becoming aware of what stresses you and why. Stress is not uniform across people. The thought of the same activity will not necessarily affect two people the same way unless they have the same beliefs about that activity. It is so easy to live without questioning why you believe what you do. I believe we are all doing the best we can with what is available to us — be that our skills, time, energy, or resources; simply learning where you gained your beliefs can provide you with new insights to propel you forward or provide opportunities for change.

The way I see it, we all have the **capacity** to possess high self-worth, feel love, wealth, and success in our lives if we truly want it. What this looks like is different for everyone, but sometimes our conditioning and beliefs prevent us from achieving the successes we desire. In addition, many of us compare to unreasonable and unachievable standards, so we don't even realize when we're achieving success. I like to remember the following when I'm comparing myself and (often) feeling dissatisfied or disappointed at myself or not being better.

"Measure against your OLD SELF, and you'll see how far you've come. This is your memory.

"Measure against a FANTASY SELF, such as someone you think you should be, and you'll probably be disappointed. This is your imagination.

"Measure against your REAL SELF, and you'll see you're 100% identical, therefore perfect. This is the person reading this text right now and the only actual version of you that exists."

Comfort Zones

I was in a street market in Thailand several years ago with my friend, Andrew, and we came across a stall selling fried crickets, roasted grub worms, and fried scorpions. Knowing my penchant for stepping outside my comfort zone, Andrew offered to buy me a scorpion on a stick, as long as I would eat it! Up until that point in my life, I had consumed some strange foods, but a large, mean-looking black scorpion on a skewer was not in my repertoire, yet I accepted. Anyone *could* eat a scorpion (the stinger was removed, and the venom was cooked out of it, so it was harmless), but only some people would be willing to. What determines who would be open to that opportunity?

When we are born, we don't have any frame of reference for the world; we are purely stimulus/response creatures. As we gain experience, we learn what we like and don't like what we are willing and able to do, and what is outside our reach. Anything we're willing to do easily is within our comfort zone, and when we remain inside this zone, life is very safe and more consistent. Unfortunately, the downside of this is that we slow our growth potential by staying there. It's not that we need to constantly be moving outside our comfort zone, but it is important to be aware that on the edge of support and challenge is where we grow most effectively. If we want change, we have to be willing to step out.

"A comfort zone is a self-imposed limitation."

Although outside influences can lead us to create our comfort zone, we are the ones who guard and enforce it. Like a noisy duck whose quack sounds like an omnipresent complaint, if it doesn't like its situation, it can spread its wings and fly away. There is a societal pressure that leads us to stay consistent with our identity. This reinforces in people a desire to remain in their comfort zones. That belief is just a norm to help us feel safe, but it's also a boundary designed to be expanded if you want more from your life.

The next diagram is a representation of a comfort zone. I have used food as the example topic, and, as you can see, there is a range of items that Sally would be comfortable eating. Again, it doesn't mean she likes those items, but if she had to, she'd consume them. Given normal circumstances, Sally would not touch something outside her comfort zone, so sushi, oysters, eyeballs, and scorpions are not an option.

Sally's comfort zone = what she is willing to eat.

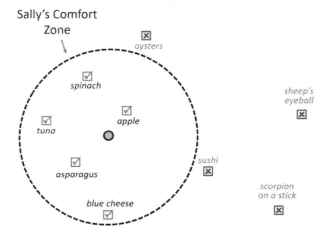

Imagine Sally is on vacation on a beach in Mauritius, and there's nothing but oysters to eat, caught fresh from the sea, and everyone else is eating them at a lovely beach party. We can assume she may try one if she were in the spirit of being on vacation or even if she were just really hungry. Alternatively, Sally could be having a meal with someone she really admired or was trying to impress, and that person loved oysters and offered her one to try. Depending on how far outside her comfort zone oysters were and how important the person was to her, it is possible she would try one. She may or may not like it, but if she did decide to try it, something magical would happen—her comfort zone would expand, as is indicated on the drawing below.

Sally's expanded comfort zone after trying something new.

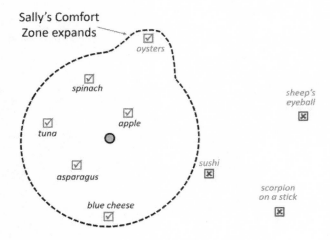

This diagram is only illustrative, however, when we step outside our comfort zone and achieve something we never thought was possible, we build our self-belief, and our confidence grows. We can see there was something Sally thought was not possible, and now it's possible. The effect is to push out the boundaries. You can see what happens on the chart on the next page. It's quite remarkable!

And there's more...

Think of your comfort zone as a bubble. When it expands in one direction, there's also an expansion in other, unrelated areas. Confidence doesn't care if you're trying food, asking for a pay rise, or speaking to a stranger; the sense of trust confidence gives you is content free — it will work in any area. It's not always easy to identify the link; however, there are things you have done in your life which were only available to you because of a fear you overcame in another area. My willingness to try new and unusual foods may be linked to the fact I have traveled so much: my confidence in travel has led to an increased comfort zone of foods I'm willing to try.

Check out how much Sally has expanded her comfort zone now!

Sally's new comfort zone after natural expansion.

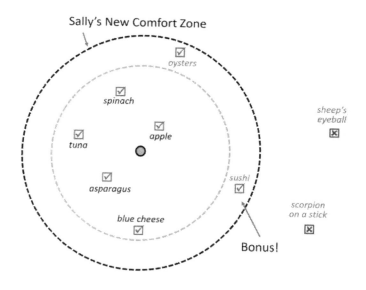

Whenever you notice yourself holding back from doing something you feel could be supportive and beneficial, take a look at the beliefs you have relating to it. Not having done something has no correlation as to whether you *can* do it. [12]

---

[12] *On a side note, I'd like to mention that I chose the food examples specifically because I have tried them all – my comfort zone is pretty large, which provides me flexibility in life no matter the situation from strange food to no food.*

> ***"You can do things you can't even imagine."***
>
> I gave two Spanish circus performers a ride up the east coast of Australia once, and they told me a story of their travels to the country of Laos, which is next to Cambodia. They were in a minority village high in the hills where the locals had seen hardly any foreigners before. As they played with the children, showing them sights they'd never seen before, they pulled out their juggling balls, and many of the children tried this new skill of juggling. One girl watched quietly until she was handed the balls. With no effort whatsoever, she threw the balls in the air and juggled perfectly.

Your conditioning can be the result of others' injected values and beliefs into your life. These may have evolved over years or been instilled in a short timeframe. When you ask yourself how you developed a certain belief and how that belief serves you, you'll get to know yourself better. When you ask *why*, your brain goes straight to justification, whereas by asking *how* your mind goes to the evidence to support your belief. Once you get answers, it's up to you if you want to keep that belief or upgrade it. As that happens, your self-trust and confidence grow, and you achieve more when you enter an upward spiral.

"How do I have this belief and how does it serve me?"

So far, we've looked at how Conditioning and Comfort Zones affect your Internal Confidence, which is your ability to believe you can achieve something. Now we're going to talk about self-belief.

Self-belief

My Australian girlfriend, Kelly, and I were driving up to the immigration booth in Dover on our way to board the Cross-Channel ferry to France from England some years ago when I made a startling realization. That morning I had spontaneously suggested to Kelly, who was on a working holiday in the UK, that we take a day trip to France. We packed our things, met up, and in no time, were winging our way down to the coast, looking forward to red wine, fresh baguettes, and Camembert. At the time, the UK was part of the European Union, and as I have lived in France and speak French, I completely overlooked the fact that I'd need a passport to get into the country. Not getting past the immigration booth at this point would ruin our day. When I understood the challenge, I reached deep inside and took a healthy dose of self-confidence.

I've seen *Crocodile Dundee* and *Star Wars* and know about Jedi mind tricks. I made a decision at that moment that my driver's license would be fine as an ID document, and that I would do what I could to convey that message to the woman in the booth.

> *"Passports, please."*

> *"Here's my driver's license, and my girlfriend is visiting from Australia, so here's her passport."*

> The passport officer took and inspected our documents.

> *"I'll need your passport."*

> *"It's okay. I'm a British citizen. My driver's license will be fine. My license is fine."*

After some idle banter (not about the license), she let us through. I had such a high level of confidence and self-belief that my license would be fine that the woman accepted what I had to say. I'd never done this before, yet in that moment threw off my societal conditions and stepped distinctly out of my comfort zone. I did use other conversation skills to my advantage; however, my belief I could succeed with this plan was the foundation of the solution, and we had a wonderful day trip in France.

I'm not suggesting you use these Jedi mind tricks today as an immigration tactic; I just wanted to illustrate that when you have a solid level of self-belief, you can achieve things you never thought were even possible. If you had asked me to prepare for that situation, I don't know what I'd have done, but I had enough awareness of my conditioning, a willingness to stretch my comfort zones, and self-belief in my skills, that I went for it.

Just to be clear, the worst-case scenario would have been that we were turned back to stay in the UK, and we'd lose our ferry tickets, but in the moment, it felt very intense.

Here's an excerpt from an article I wrote entitled:

Your Best Friend and Your Worst Enemy

There's somebody you see every day, but chances are you don't really know them. You may not think of them as a friend, and to be honest, you often treat them worse than your worst enemy. You talk to them interminably, but frequently only to chastise, berate or criticize their behavior and clothes, the way they look, the things they do and the life they're leading. It is likely you have extremely high standards for this person, but if you were asked to write them down, you'd find it difficult to do. Nevertheless, you expect them to live by these unwritten rules.

Need I say more? Have you worked out who it is? Listen...they just spoke to you.

Can you hear me? Yes, it's you. YOU! Your best friend in the universe thinks you're so awesome that they've chosen to be a part of you. In fact, they're never going to leave you. No matter what you do, they will always be with you. Stop. Listen, and appreciate that little voice — your best friend is talking to you.

What are the foundations of your belief?

"Look at how much you've achieved.
Seriously, you're pretty awesome
but may just have forgotten..."

We aren't always nice to ourselves. We often magnify our faults and downplay our attributes, which is detrimental to our self-esteem. It's hard to get away when you're beating yourself up on the inside.

Whether you realize it or not, you have achieved so much in your life. With all the dangers in the world today, from disease to crime, to bad luck, you have managed not to die from...well, anything. If you are reading this sentence, you have survived **every single life experience** that has been thrown at you: you're pretty incredible.

Reflecting on what you have already achieved gives you a free resource to change your state and improve your self-belief. Grab a pen or start a new document — time for a fun exercise!

You're about to remember how much you've achieved. I know you're going to get excited, but before you start, read the following question and give yourself a score from 1-10 for your current self-belief. Choose any number that feels right and note it down.

Question: On a scale of 1-10, how likely are you to accomplish your next clear goal?

When You Appreciate, You Appreciate Exercise

Although we relate to ourselves as one being, we're really a collection of everything we've experienced and done or not done. With so much going on in life, seldom do we reflect on how far we've progressed, and there is a wealth of energy there to propel us today if we focus on it. The energy comes in many forms, one of which is dopamine. Dopamine is responsible for the feel-good energy we have when we achieve something or cross something off our to-do list. Our brains are so fantastic, brain scans have shown that we can actually experience a similar dopamine response from our bodies just by reflecting on things we've achieved, which is why this exercise is important. Look at the things you've done through inquisitive eyes.

It is great practice to write down these ideas, and if you were to come up with a list of 100 answers of what you've achieved in your life, it would have a profound effect on you.

But I know you're a busy person. Well, if you're not going to write these down, spend seven minutes somewhere quietly thinking about the answers in each area. You may even feel inspired to make notes after all, but either way, this exercise will have an impact.

Steps:

1. Your aim is to write down 100 things you've achieved or done in life, focusing on things that make you feel successful.

2. You are judging your replies, so if you like the idea, write it down. Aim to get a range of answers in different parts of life. Remember that sometimes the things we feel are our biggest achievements may not be known or witnessed by others, so be sure to reflect on them, such as going through a relationship break-up well.

Think of all you have learned. Can you use a dishwasher, make macaroni and cheese? Think of all the subjects you learned at school and any assignments you've ever done. Consider all you've done for friends, your community, your family. What jobs have you had? What skills do you have? Can you tie your shoelaces, can you speak iPhone and Android, have you ever taken a good photo you loved? Think of all the money you've ever saved — or spent! Or, the number of YouTube videos you've watched or TV series you've binged. How many pizzas you've eaten, or books you've read, have you helped a stranger, asked for directions in a foreign country, sewed a button, solved a riddle, nailed something together, been there for a friend, held someone in silence, bought someone a coffee, given an awesome gift, seen a play, learned about animals, used VR (virtual reality), sent a letter, said no at the right time, paid for groceries, won a prize or pretty much anything you can think of? Have you ever raised money for a cause, fixed a problem using the internet, baked a cake, created life, given birth, driven a car, camped, built anything, entertained children, passed an exam or test, earned a wage, been to another state, held a snake, traveled overseas, tied a tie, worn heels all night, made breakfast in bed for someone, given flowers, had a pay raise, been complimented? And so on...

There is also a range of things you've achieved by NOT doing something. For example, many of us have learned to apologize for our mistakes, kept fit and healthy—avoiding unnecessary illnesses, not been a smoker, not used unnecessary physical force in a situation, not had our way so someone else could succeed, not continued a family trait we felt was important to let go of, or any of a range of things where we sacrificed our needs for another or stopped doing something we felt was unnecessary.

This is supposed to be a fun exercise, so start noting things down. Use any of the suggestions above and add to them. There are no rules, so write it if you like it.

Consider answers in the following areas: physical, financial, social, family, relationship, mental, spiritual, or use your different feeds, apps, websites, and photo albums for inspiration.

After you have written the list:

Once you have completed your list of 100 things you have achieved, take a moment to reflect on it. Whilst sitting in a quiet place, take long, comfortable breaths as you re-read each of the things you've achieved. Give yourself some time to remember how much you've impacted people, how much you've grown, and how much you've touched people.

Once you've reflected for a few minutes, answer the following question:

Question: On a scale of 1-10, how likely are you to accomplish your next clear goal?

Many people feel a higher level of confidence that they can achieve something after they reflect on what they've achieved so far.

Remember, comparing yourself to others is not an effective scale because you don't know all the conditions of someone else's situation. Compare to a previous version of you when you were younger, and you'll see how far you've come. Keep in mind that the real you is the only version of you who actually exists...the other versions are figments of your or other people's imaginations in the future and past.

The purpose of this exercise is to remind you of your abilities and help you shed some limiting beliefs you may have about who you are. In the next section, we'll look at how you convert Internal Confidence into power by the way you interact with the world through External Confidence.

Success and Gratitude List

I recommend using a note on your phone or a small book to record your successes when you have them. If you're ever feeling low, remember your note or read a few pages as it will really inspire you. Some people use a list like this to guide them in what to be grateful for and reflect on sections of a gratitude list before going to bed. This is a great idea because feelings of gratitude carry over into your body, help you heal, and improve your sleep.

"Whether you think you can,
or you think you can't – you're right."
Henry Ford

"Success is something you magnetically attract by becoming an attractive person."

In conclusion, Internal Confidence is made up of your Conditioning, Comfort Zones, and Self-belief, all of which you can change with focused effort. Improving in any of these areas improves our ability to take action.

External Confidence

The areas previously mentioned are more focused on our internal perspectives; however, confidence is a currency of connection in both work and play. After working on our internal muscles, it's time to reach out to the world and connect.

I split External Confidence into two primary areas:

- **Appearance**: how people perceive you based on your look and behavior
- **Interaction**: your ability to connect with others

These relate to our external appearance and interaction skills. The ways in which I define these are as follows:

Appearance and Interaction Model

Appearance

This is the information we convey to the world about how we physically look and how our clothes and bodies appear.

Many people have had no guidance in regard to their appearance, or no longer pay it much attention.

- Understanding yourself allows you to make quality clothing decisions.

- You never get a second chance to make a first impression and understanding how people perceive you gives you the ability to achieve more.

- The way you look and feel affects your confidence levels.

- The right look attracts the right kind of people.

Interaction

Our ability to interact with others affects what we can achieve in life. With the right attitude and skills, the most amazing achievements are possible, as these provide us with clarity and direction regarding what is important and the skills to connect to achieve more. The skills in interaction allow you to:

- Connect with strangers more easily.

- Better understand others and overcome fear.

- Feel and behave more authentically.

Once you're attracting and connecting with people, use your Internal Confidence to build great relationships and wealth in all areas of your life.

External Confidence involves a much more practical set of skills that you can learn and practice. Although we can survive on our own, we thrive when others are around us. The human experience is magnified by relationships, and External Confidence helps us create those connections. It should be remembered, though, that although External Confidence is what creates relationships, it is the foundation of Internal Confidence that leads to ongoing success in connecting with others. It's important to work on both parts to become more skillful and fulfilled.

Confidence is both visible and invisible.

I used to study aikido in Los Angeles and had an excellent teacher, Lia Suzuki Sensei. I loved aikido because the art of *aligning* and *redirecting* an attack also works with energy and words. In addition to regular classes, other sensei from around the world would visit for workshops. Recently, I participated in an aikido demonstration at a sales training for resistance-free selling.

When my sensei was a grasshopper black belt, she was giving her first class as a teacher, and as the students knelt watching her, she demonstrated a technique on one of them. Mid-move, she paused to explain what she was doing. As she was talking, she suddenly sensed her right leg shaking uncontrollably, due to nerves, and she cringed inside at the thought of her lack of confidence showing so overtly. Her confidence level at that moment was probably pretty low.

Nevertheless, she continued her explanation, and as she was talking and gesturing, her eyes caught sight of the offending leg. It was at that moment she realized that her hakama (baggy black aikido trousers for black belts) was covering her legs in such a way that nobody could see the shaking! At that moment, her confidence level rocketed back up, and she left that class with her honor intact and a great lesson:

"You decide your own confidence."

Just as comfort zones are self-imposed limitations, your self-confidence in any situation is governed by your beliefs. You can certainly learn skills to help you boost your ability to connect with others, and I have split these into two sections: Appearance and Interaction.

1. Appearance

I am no style guru, but I understand the effect of appearance on how we're perceived, so please understand that I'm just providing some foundational ideas for those who haven't considered them before. There are many factors that determine how we are perceived by others, and understanding the messages you are sending gives you a greater ability to influence.

Think about the last time you were wearing clothes you really liked, maybe for a special occasion. Or recall a time where you were complimented on how you looked. It is likely that your level of confidence increased as a result of these external factors. Although temporary, these influences can boost your confidence in a moment and give you more resources to deal with a situation. If we consider the dating or business arenas, this kind of edge can make the difference between striking up a conversation or getting the deal.

Whether someone is confident or not, they can give an air of confidence without even opening their mouth. It could be the way they dress, the way they stand, the way they look, or even the movements they make. In this section, we'll cover a range of valuable insights to show you how to give an air of confidence even before you speak.

Do Your Clothes Suit You?

I remember working in a huge multinational in Australia and was proud of the fact I turned up every day in a smart, well-ironed shirt and trousers. One day out of the blue, one of my friends in the office asked me if I deliberately wore oversized clothes or if there was another reason that I wore the clothes I did. I was surprised, as I'd thought I had good style, but when I checked, I could see that my shirt *was* a bit baggy around the body. The shirt was well-made and of good quality. On the hanger, it looked great. But because of the shape of my body, the excess material was sack-like on me and made me look bigger. It was a similar situation with the trousers.

The day my friend mentioned my look, she showed me my reflection. I looked in the mirror and realized that I had a kind of 80's baggy clothes style that wasn't really fashionable. I had never looked at myself that way, although I'd seen myself in the mirror thousands of times. This reflection made me change my style, and I noticed a considerable boost in my confidence when I started wearing clothes that suited me.

Another monumental moment around style happened when I saw a photo of myself as a teenager and noticed that the glasses I wore absolutely didn't suit my face. I wore those glasses for years and never even considered I could get a different pair. I really believe that my popularity and confidence would have been greatly enhanced had I worn more appropriately styled glasses, even in those formative years.

These experiences made me aware of my look in a way I hadn't considered before. Although it depends on your generation and peers, many of us have not had guidance around clothes and style. If you have, you may be aware of the tips I'm talking about, and this next section might not be as useful to you, but it's still worth a read.

Often, we confuse style with cost or buy into the latest trends, fashions, and colors without considering if they suit us. The clothes we wear and the way we wear them have a big impact on the way people perceive us — they're like the headline for a show.

Clothing Basics

This section is designed to bring your attention to some key areas of your appearance. Some points may sound obvious, but check yourself that you're following the simple guidelines.

Whether male, female or trans, the guidance relates to how traditionally we feel about clothing worn by people being perceived to be that sex. This is now evolving; however, many people will still follow these stereotypes.

Ensure your clothes and shoes are clean and tidy.

- This is something we all can do. If you have stains or rips in your clothes or shoes, missing buttons, frayed threads, or anything else which is not deliberate, consider repairing or replacing the items. And take time to iron clothes which should be wrinkle-free.

Ensure you and your clothes are fresh and smell appropriate.

- If you've ever spoken to someone who had a strong smell, you know how little attention you paid to the conversation. This also includes too much perfume or aftershave; even if someone smells good, too much is too much.

Accessories

Men are often judged by their phones, watches, and similar items such as pens; Women tend to be judged by their hair and shoes — keep this in mind when creating your outfit. If you want to see this theory in action, notice how you feel when these items are incongruent in someone you're with. Examples could be a guy in a smart suit who uses a chewed pen to sign a document or a woman in a beautiful dress with dirty shoes.

Shoes

To give the best impression, ensure you keep your shoes in good condition (scuffs can be dealt with using a little polish or even coconut oil) and wipe off any built-up dirt. Heels should not be noticeably worn, and a quick visit to a cobbler can repair your favorite shoes. The style of shoe will determine how important this is, but remember it's the little things that can make a big difference. There's a saying that:

"How we do one thing is often how we do anything."

So, if someone sees you pay attention to the details, they'll unconsciously assume you do the same in other areas.

Watches and Pens

If you choose to wear a watch, a slimline classic Roman numeral watch says something very different than a chunky or digital one. If you like your smartwatch, consider the option of a hybrid smartwatch, which has an analog face but still tracks your health and more.

Imagine how you'd feel if you were about to sign an important contract and were handed a cheap, plastic pen to close the deal. I'm sure you can imagine this would be a very different experience compared to being handed a slim, stylish metal pen. You don't need to spend a lot on a pen, but keep an eye out for one with a classic look you like and use it regularly instead of a plastic one.

Body

Your health supports you in everything you do, so maintain and improve your system by learning about it and healthy foods. Being healthy is not rocket science: include a combination of quality fruits, vegetables, grains, and nuts in your diet and minimize additional sugar. Also, keep active and get a reasonable amount of sleep as this provides the environment for your body to heal and expel toxins. These things will all assist you in feeling better, which translates as appearing and feeling more confident in yourself and toward others.

Remember to pay attention to some of the little things — keep yourself clean and tidy regarding skin, teeth, nails, hair, eyes, and breath.

2. Interaction

When interacting with others, our confidence is improved when we know what to say. The way we say something is also very important, and the essence of that can be conveyed through our authenticity, which is what we'll cover in this section.

(The final section of the 3Cs model provides specific phrases and words to use to start, maintain and close conversations. These practical tools are amplified through communicating authentically.)

How Do Authentic People Communicate?

Authentic means that something is not a copy; it is genuine or true. When we speak with authenticity, we share what's really going on with us to the best of our ability, as opposed to what we think other people want to hear. When we project an *image* of who we think we are onto others, instead of sharing who we *actually* are, there's a greater margin for confusion and miscommunication.

Lying takes soooo much energy...

I remember a conversation with a friend about how stressful it was to tell lies. I'd not considered the energy used to tell lies before that conversation, and it helped me realize how much of my power was being drained by being dishonest. I was in my late teens and lived just north of London at the time. At school, I had multiple groups of friends, and every time I told a story, I'd have to remember what I'd said to whom, and that took up so much space in my mind. Over time, I untied the web of misinformation I'd spread and learned to be honest or be quiet.

"I'm not upset because you lied, I'm sad that I can't trust you anymore."

I share these thoughts on dishonesty to inform you of that valuable lesson...lying is stressful, time-consuming, and is generally going to cost you. People *can* handle the truth, and authentic people convey themselves truthfully. The benefit of being honest is that you don't need to keep track of alternate versions of reality or waste energy stressing, both of which age you unnecessarily due to the additional oxidation they create in your system. If you've stretched the truth a bit in the past, let it go and focus on communicating more honestly, going forward. You may find it challenging in the short term; however, the benefits of communicating authentically far outweigh the downsides.

Many of us have not been communicating authentically due to a fear of how others will perceive us. Try some of the following suggestions, which will help loosen some of your beliefs and give you the resource of flexibility. This isn't always an easy path, but it is a worthy one.

When communicating authentically, here are some ideas to keep in mind:

Speak Honestly and with Compassion

The way you deliver information makes a huge difference. Being honest does not mean being arrogant or brash. If someone asks for your opinion about something you dislike, there's no need to be rude in your response. My mother used to say, *"If you can't say something nice, don't say anything at all."* If you must respond, focus on the things you do like about the person or the situation so you can be honest.

You are always free to change your mind, so share your opinion when asked and qualify it with an appropriate phrase such as:

- *Right now, I feel that...*

- *In my opinion...*

- *Hypothetically...*

Share Some of Yourself

It's wonderful to see people open up when you find a mutual interest, and the way to do that is to share something that interests you. My wife is an avid orchid cultivator, and the pleasure she gets when she meets others with a similar interest is such a joy to watch. She has hosted orchid-mounting tea parties, where a group comes to our house and takes a tour in the greenhouse before enjoying an orchid-mounting class in the gazebo and afternoon tea. I help out as she leads the day.

- Did you notice what I just did? I sneakily shared some of me with you to illustrate this point. As a result, there might be a change in how you perceive me now, and that is a direct result of me sharing some of myself. When you get excited about something in life, feel free to share it with people, and ask questions if they have similar passions.

Does Anything Need to Be Said at All?

Keep in mind that if you don't feel like talking, you don't have to. We're all so caught up with filling the void that we're missing out on the value of quiet, reflection, and even boredom. A balanced life is the most fulfilling, so it's okay to speak sometimes and at other times to remain silent.

Use the phrases and tools from the communication chapter as you share more of yourself authentically.

Be sure to check out the exercise section for ways to practice these skills. There will come a time where you'll naturally employ many more of these skills.

Fear and How to Fail

Many people fear failure and agree it is a feeling they generally want to avoid. A common mistake we make is to create intentions and beliefs about how things should turn out (usually based on fantasies instead of realities), and when they don't go exactly that way, we can feel like a failure.

The irony of failure is that we often create an image in our minds of what happens when we try new things, which is based on childhood or early adulthood experiences that are no longer valid. What if those exact situations happened today? It might be standing up and reading a poem in a class of nine-year-olds. When you originally read that poem as a nine-year-old, you were laughed at, but now you would be far more capable of dealing with the situation. **The fear, therefore, is not based on our actual experience; it is based on an extrapolation of a childhood fear and how we feel we should behave today as an adult**. Our fear of fear can sometimes be greater than the experience itself.

When I was younger and living in Hong Kong, I decided I wasn't good at reading out loud. I felt my voice was boring, and I made lots of mistakes. I remember that horrible feeling of waiting to be asked to stand up and read something in class, and that feeling, and fear, stayed with me up to and beyond university. **If I'd understood the message of fear earlier (which was, *get prepared*)**, I could have acted on the signal and taken action to build my confidence and overcome my fear by gaining more experience, knowledge, and practice. Then I wouldn't have had to carry that specific fear for so many years, which I know impacted my confidence. Remember: *life's delays are not life's denials.* Sometimes when we think something bad has happened and we're not getting our way, we are actually being prepared for something else.

My parents are great cooks. I have been blessed with an upbringing of weird and wonderful flavors and foods prepared by them in my life from Indonesian spareribs, to Moroccan lamb and prune tagine to micro-sliced pineapple deserts and flaming Christmas pudding so as I grew up I watched and learned how they created these dishes. My brother and I did cook with my parents sometimes, but my ability to cook today has come from my willingness to mix foods, taste them and learn from all the delicious and quite disastrous meals I've made. I once made a big batch of cupcakes, including truffles and saffron...not a single cake was edible!

I built my confidence in many areas of my life one experience at a time, and because I've had to deal with potentially failing, I now have a reduced fear of failure.

Confident People Fail the Most

Confident people fail the most because they have developed their failure muscle. Are you developing this muscle?

It's a fact that confident people fail far more frequently simply because they try things more frequently. My ability to be confident in incredibly diverse situations is fundamentally based on the fact that I've succeeded and failed thousands of times at many of the things I've tried — and I've been okay with that. It is my ability to look confident despite how I feel inside that I know has built my confidence and ability to attract what I want in the world. I absolutely recommend understanding the rules of External Confidence and attraction to anyone wanting to grow their self-worth and build their self-esteem.

Separate the Behavior from the Person

There is nothing wrong with failing, and the most successful people in the world fail far more frequently than those who don't try. You've no doubt heard stories of great inventors such as Edison and the light bulb; he failed thousands of times before getting it right. His behavior led to success but was littered with disappointment. When we brand a person with a label, the label has a lot of power, and if we consider ourselves a failure, that can be very hard to deal with. Do your best to see that we all have behaviors that succeed and fail, but they are separate from who we are. This is particularly important with children who may behave poorly but are good kids behaving badly as opposed to bad kids.

I would suggest that, in some circumstances, it is healthy to expect to fail because to fail, you have to try. When it comes to dating, a lot of people complain about not having a partner, but they're not asking anybody on a date or taking action to meet people. Knowing how to break the ice and ask people on dates can seem daunting because we have to deal with rejection head-on, however, by learning and practicing what to do and taking small, semi-comfortable steps, anybody can be successful in meeting people.

I have so much respect for individuals who take consistent steps toward something important to them, whatever it is. A disciple[13] is disciplined and consistently learns and practices, and it is healthy to be a disciple of our own lives.

Somewhere along the line, failure was given a bad name, and we were taught that it should be avoided at all costs, but the sooner we realize that failure is an integral part of any successful person's life, then we'll release the stranglehold it has on us. **Success is not possible without failure.**

Dealing with Rejection

If we feel rejected, it often means we had an expectation that wasn't met and are experiencing a sense of loss. The question

---

[13] *Disciple comes from the Latin discere meaning to learn.*

to ask ourselves is, *have we really lost anything?* Sometimes we haven't communicated our feelings or wishes, and the person isn't rejecting us; they're just focused on something else. If we make a point of checking in with that person and telling them in a way they can hear what our expectations are, that can improve the situation by creating clarity. Sometimes they will be able to help; sometimes they won't... Either way, the act of being heard helps us feel better.

> **People don't have to have their way;**
> **they have to have their say.**

If they can't help, maybe we will have to find another way to satisfy that need inside ourselves.

I was on a long road trip in Australia with a girlfriend, and she was on her phone all the time, which made me feel unimportant. I did feel rejected at times, but I also knew that she had affairs to attend to and organize. I asked her if she could help me feel more connected, and I explained how I felt. She was great, and we worked out a solution where she would just tell me what she was organizing in her business or who she was chatting with, and as a result, I felt like I was a part of the conversation. I also realized I had my own things to think about, so I pondered, listened to the music and enjoyed the drive.

Rejection by Your Peers

A funny thing happens, often subconsciously, to people around us when they see us start to change. They sometimes become worried that we're going to get disappointed if we fail and so they guide us back to old habits. Other times, they're worried about how they're going to deal with the new you, because they've never actually met that person. These and other concerns are natural and healthy. It's equally natural and healthy to listen to opinions and feedback from others then make decisions that support you to become the best you can be for yourself and others. That way, we all win.

It's not all good when you're more confident. As you can see, confidence has two sides. When you build your confidence and start to take steps toward outcomes that are important to you, it's inevitable you will receive resistance.

Unwanted Attention

You may also get unwanted attention as you build your confidence or have to deal with uncomfortable situations. Well, that's the kind of thing a confident person can deal with. Whenever you are in an uncomfortable situation, quickly ask yourself...

"What do I want instead?"

...and take action toward the answer. Keep yourself safe and remember to be clear about what outcome you want at any moment so you will have the greatest chance of your goals coming to fruition.

Once, a friend from overseas visited me in Australia and stayed at my place. When we had a falling out, I decided he had to leave. I had to ask him to vacate my house knowing he didn't have friends nearby and didn't know the city. It was one of the hardest things I've had to do, and it built my confidence muscle dramatically as well as my comfort zone because I didn't know how he would react. All I knew was that I had to stand up for what was important to me.

*"Confidence is built through experience.
To build your experience, regularly
learn and try new things."*

You may feel overwhelmed at the array of ideas I've given you: however, fear not, as working on even one of them from any section, will have an impact on your confidence. At the end of the book is a section entitled Inspiring Menus. These are some suggested plans of action to take to help improve your confidence. Try some for a week or two and notice the changes.

There is also such a thing as *too much confidence*. When we feel a lack of something, such as if we were crawling through a desert dehydrated in the burning sun, we may fantasize that having oceans of water to quench our thirst would be a good thing; however, once our thirst was quenched, the additional water wouldn't help us and could, in fact, be a problem. Here's an unfortunate story where I learned about having too much confidence.

Too Much Confidence Nearly Cost Me My Right Arm

Here's a crazy story to remind you of the balance in life:

It was 2 pm on Valentine's Day, and I was dancing on a hill in the sun at a festival four hours northwest of Brisbane, Australia. I love going to festivals and often find myself at them because to do so satisfies my highest values.

And then it happened... I was knocked unconscious when I fell down the sloping dance floor and landed on my shoulder and head. Just before the incident, I had been sitting next to the stage, taking a breather. As I stood quickly and walked up the sloping dance floor, I didn't anticipate the magnitude of the headrush I would experience, and as I tried to steady myself, I stumbled and hit the deck. For a moment, I didn't know where I was, but after I made my way out of the sun, I took stock of what had happened.

I was a bit shaken up and noticed my right arm felt different. I wasn't wearing a shirt, and as I looked from my hand to my elbow and then to my shoulder, I noticed a protruding shape under the skin near my collarbone. It was surprising that there was no pain, and I concluded that I must have dislocated my shoulder. I've only ever seen a dislocated shoulder portrayed in movies, so it was pure guesswork on my part. In hindsight, the fact there was no pain is a strong indicator that it wasn't dislocated!

As an advocate of self-care and confident in my ability to deal with my own body, I decided I would fix this situation as quickly as possible to avoid the muscles and tissue swelling, thus making this "dislocation" harder to deal with. I approached the other festivalgoers and stallholders and asked them to help me relocate my shoulder. Only one guy was willing, but he didn't know what to do, so I didn't take his offer because I didn't, either.

Eventually, I made my way to the First Aid area, and an extremely overweight and unhealthy-looking nurse said he'd help me. He told me I should have it X-rayed in case there was anything broken. But I told him I knew it was dislocated, and I needed it worked on immediately so I could get back to my day. My confidence about what was required was so high; I wouldn't listen to him. I left First Aid and asked another fifteen people for help, to no avail. In the end, I returned to the medic and accepted the headache pill and sling the nurse offered. We had a long journey ahead of us back to civilization, and the first 12km involved driving on dirt tracks. So we all got into our cars and followed each other in convoy, heading back to Brisbane.

Four hours later, we arrived in the emergency department of a Brisbane hospital, and I was quickly ushered in to see a doctor to whom I explained my story. I must have seemed confident, persuasive, and believable, since he accepted my diagnosis and, within a moment, he was relocating my arm! If you've seen *Die Hard* when Bruce Willis runs into a door frame to relocate his shoulder, you'll know that a massive amount of pressure is required to fix this situation. I was amazed at how the doctor manipulated and rotated my arm for the next thirty seconds; above my head, out to the side, backward and then with full force, he snapped it down by my side and looked at me with a smile, proud of his handiwork.

"How does that feel now?" he asked.

"It feels fine, but it never used to look like that," I replied as I pointed at the protrusion I'd noticed earlier. He looked perplexed for a moment, then said, "Hmmm... we'd better get you some X-rays..."

It turned out I had snapped my collarbone in a particularly awkward way (which has now been beautifully rectified with a little surgery), and I've since considered that the treatment I was initially given could have ended up making the situation a lot worse — with the possibility of the adjustment leading to permanent disability if the sharp bone had severed a tendon!

I share this story to remind you that, like all things, confidence at the wrong time can be a disadvantage. Building your confidence is important, but knowing when to use it is equally important.

> *"Being too confident in a dangerous situation can literally end in death. Use this powerful tool wisely."*

Chapter 5: Clear Direction

Firstly, we'll cover **why it's important to have some direction** in your life and how to make that happen to **clear out tasks and move forward** with your current wants and needs. Next, we'll look at how you can use Clear Direction, together with clarifying your values to **determine what is truly important to you**. Then we'll cover **how to use the advantages of momentum** and, finally, we'll talk about the kinds of **things which may hold you back and how to overcome them**.

I have been to markets across the world, from dusty gem stalls in Rubyvale or the extensive Eumundi markets on the Sunshine Coast in Australia to the Jemaa el-Fnaa souk in Marrakesh and the Grande Bazar in Istanbul. I thoroughly enjoyed visiting all of them with their spicy local foods, fresh leather goods, hand-carved wood, silver treasures, snake charmers, dangerous dive bars, world-class buskers, and charming street cats. Some were certainly maze-like, but during my excursions, I always managed to make my way home, despite how deeply I explored. When I visited these markets, I didn't specifically have a path to leave them; however, I always knew the next few steps toward home. Whether that meant heading back to the entrance, down the hill, or simply calling an Uber, knowing my next three steps have made a world of difference in the flow of my life.

Life is a journey, not a destination, so Clear Direction does not mean knowing and focusing on the final destination (which, ironically, we don't really want because it is the cemetery), it means knowing the path forward. The next three steps. That's all. Life is a whirlwind already, and many of us are just trying to hang on, so I encourage you to simply be aware of the next three steps in anything you're doing when you want to feel direction. The more skilled you are at using this method, the longer you'll be able to handle knowing what to do in the next ten minutes, all the way up to the next ten years.

WHY Is It important to Have Direction?

Save for a few moments when I was on a walkabout in Australia and New Zealand with no connection to anything, I have always had things to do. Always. It is a misguided belief held by many people that there will come a point where we'll have done all the things on our to-do list, and we'll finally be able to relax. My experience is that this is not true, so I have embraced the belief there will always be things to do and focused on managing those tasks to the best of my ability. Although a simple concept, this is really no easy task with the deluge of activities and distractions spiraling around us constantly trying to get our attention.

"Without a vision, the people perish."

Many of us prepare more for a one-week holiday than we do for the rest of the year. We often have a plan for the travel arrangements, the key activities we're going to be doing, a budget of what we can spend, and all the details scheduled for our safe return home.

Imagine what your year would be like if you had a simple and easy plan.

Just like a holiday plan, it's flexible, but it gives you an outline to follow. All you need to know is the next step to assist you in taking action toward a want or goal, which helps create momentum.

"When you have no direction, you can have all the resources in the world and achieve nothing."

This simplest plan is all you need to get started, which is usually the hardest step. In writing this book, I didn't know exactly how I would convey the ideas I wanted to share, but I knew I had to start writing it. Once I did, I saw it coming together. As Wayne Dyer said:

"You'll see it when you believe it."
Wayne Dyer

There are major advantages to knowing and starting to take the next three steps toward anything important in your life. With a little forward planning, you can achieve so much despite the whirlwind of activities around you. This helps build your certainty and confidence by giving you a clearer idea of what time you have available and your priorities in life — which, in turn, helps many people put down their devices and focus.

With direction and a little action, you can move toward achieving anything... Write a book, land a new job, get fit, make more money, learn a skill, start a savings plan, break up with someone, start a new business or a family...anything!

Before the First Step

Whether landing a person on the moon or asking for a date from someone you don't know well, the first thing that is required for these things to be possible is that someone needs to decide.

The Burning Man festival is one of my favorite worldwide experiences. It is an art and music event set in the middle of

Black Rock Desert in Nevada, USA, whose dusty plains attract 70,000 people from around the world. Attendees build a temporary city in which to live for a week. There are no shops, and the currency is gifting, which is not to be confused with bartering, where you give with no expectation of reward other than the knowledge you helped someone. However, there are no showers, no running water, and the nearest shops are too far away to consider, except in extreme emergencies. There are no hospitals, no trash removal, and no electricity (unless you bring your own). It is dusty and hot during the day, potentially freezing at night, and if winds or a storm come through, it can be mayhem. Add rain, and it's the stickiest swampy mud you've ever dealt with! You have to provide all your own food and water and take everything out that you brought in. The mantra is: "Leave No Trace." The drive from LA, where I live, is at least eleven hours depending on stops, and the costs involved can mount easily into the thousands.

What I'm trying to convey here is that it is no easy task to prepare for and make the pilgrimage to this event, yet tens of thousands of people succeed every year.

Some people I know who are not particularly organized or motivated in daily life can turn up at an event on the other side of the planet, fully prepared to live like Mad Max for a week in a desert.

In 2013, I flew from Australia to go to the burn, which took a lot of preparation. It was there I met the incredible woman who became my wife.

So, how did I manage to plan and prepare to fly across the planet with my costumes, food, drink, transport, and accommodation needs fulfilled to live in a desert for a week?

At a high level, this is how I did it:

1. I decided I was going to go.

2. I worked out when it was feasible, considering cost and commitments, and set a date.

3. I researched how to prepare for the event by speaking to friends, watching videos, and looking online for the information I needed.

4. I identified each key area requiring preparation — plenty of lists were available online.

5. I identified key things in each area that I needed to do or get and ordered them in priority. For example, locking in flights and coordinating my work commitments.

   If a task seemed overwhelming, I broke it into smaller parts and requested help when I needed it.

6. Then I committed time weekly to the tasks and took action, reassessing, and adding to my lists as I progressed. Taking action was really easy because I was so excited about going.

Little by little, my plan came together, and the result was that I ended up in a desert in a van with food and water and somewhere to sleep. I had an incredible time at the event with a cherry on top in the form of my sweetheart! Lucky!

I've spoken to many people who are enchanted by the idea of Burning Man and have expressed that they've wanted to go for years but have never made it. There may be some valid reasons, however, for those who really want to but haven't. The primary reason is because they have yet to take the first step.

And the first step is always the same.

It happens even before you act.

The first step is quite simply to decide to do it.

Those who follow-through are the ones who tend to act immediately.

"Decision is like incision; to cut off."

When you decide to do something, you cut off the alternatives. You create power inside yourself through certainty, and your being aligns with the implications of the decision. You'll often find that once you decide something, you'll get flashes of inspiration and ideas to support the outcome you are looking for. Separated in time and size, but not in power, the tiny decision you make one day is the acorn that can become the mightiest of oaks in the future. So, remember that the first step in any journey is to decide that you're going to do it. Once you decide, take some action.

For my friends who say they want to go to Burning Man, if they've already decided to go, the next step is to simply choose the year they're going to do it (whatever feels right based on cost and commitments — this is usually 1-5 years out). For many, that's enough to get the ball rolling, and they naturally start researching how to do it and pay that goal more attention.

If you have a big task ahead, which seems insurmountable, the first step is to decide you're going to find a way to do it and then start planning by breaking it down into manageable chunks.

The First Step

As discussed, it is often the first step that is the hardest to take when embarking on a journey. It is helpful to understand why some of us feel it is difficult to take that step. The reasons can vary and are both conscious and unconscious:

- It means something is going to change.

- We perceive it will cost us energy and time.

- It is only after we take the first step that we can fail, and then we'll no longer have excuses.

- We can get judged for our actions.

- Doing what we know is so much easier.

- Shiny objects are fun, and many of us love to be distracted by immediate gratification.

Can you relate to these? I know at times in my life I've said over and over that I wanted to do something, but I didn't act on it— like the time I didn't eat for three weeks...

A few years ago, I wanted to get fitter and lose weight but wasn't doing it. Then someone at work suggested we have a 10-week Biggest Loser competition, so I took part because I enjoy competition. I started the process of eating better and going to the gym when the challenge started, which I'd wanted to do for a while but just hadn't been inspired enough. The fact that I enjoyed competition and also wanted to get fit meant it was much easier for me to begin, and the fact I was doing it with friends and colleagues supported my values even more. This illustrates how, when something is in your values, it becomes almost effortless to do.

But it didn't stop there.

After two weeks, I went to a friend's party and ate and drank outside my regimen, then didn't go to the gym for a few days. The following week I decided that it was too hard to do so much exercise and eat well for another eight weeks, but I still wanted to win, so I came up with a new strategy: I kept up with visiting the gym twice a week and also ate relatively well, but I did still eat yummy sweet things and drink alcohol. When there were three weeks left of the competition I decided to stop eating. I only drank water and had salt crystals for twenty-one days. I stepped up my exercise, too, and by the second week was running well over a marathon a week before going to work.

I won the competition, which satisfied my external needs of significance, connection, and appreciation while also fulfilling my two highest values of learning and teaching. I blogged the results and also had a number of colleagues join me for one day of fasting, too. I think our bodies are incredible, and by going through this process, I learned even more about what starvation or not eating feels like and does to us physically, mentally, and emotionally. I am also now sharing this with you, and therefore fulfilling my value of teaching.

I hope this story helps reinforce that if you can see a strong and direct connection between what you want to do and how it serves your highest values, you will act and use all the knowledge and tools you have. I know my methodology may be extreme; however, I have knowledge and experience with fasting, so I just used the resources I had. Taking time to simply write a list of how doing "x" will serve your highest values helps you create the energy to begin.

Please remember, though, that if you haven't identified the specific next steps OR the steps are too big for you to manage, that could stop you from taking action. A symptom of this is distraction.

The Next Three Steps

If you want to achieve something, identify the next three steps after starting.

Then:

1. Schedule and complete the first step.

2. Repeat.

It's so simple it sounds ridiculous, but often the simplest solutions are the best.

This method prevents overwhelm and helps guide you when you lack direction by shining a light on the next steps. It is useful for those trying to move forward with goals and equally as valuable for those trying to get their heads above water and clear out a backlog of activities. It is surprising how quickly your tasks disappear when you identify the next three steps and start taking them.

And it's a natural rush: When you achieve something, your body produces dopamine, which naturally makes you feel good. That, in turn, helps you achieve more because you're in a better state. Keeping that in mind, split bigger tasks down, so you have more to cross off. Then aim to achieve a few small pieces at a time because this helps create momentum.

To see how easy it is, let's give it a try. Think of a specific task you've been wanting to achieve, perhaps something simple you've been putting off for a while.

Once you've got it in mind, consider what the next three steps are to achieve it.

For example:

Get a new phone

1. Work out how much money I can spend (thirty mins.)

2. Research phones in stores, through friends and online (two hours)

3. Buy phone online or in-store (20/60 mins.)

Back up hard drive

1. Find backup drive or choose Cloud drive (ten mins.)

2. Set it to back up when I go to bed (ten mins.)

3. Confirm backup was successful and store backup drive if required (five mins.)

Get fit

1. Choose a fitness method and make a weekly plan (twenty-five mins.)

2. Review plan daily and follow it for a month (one min.)

3. Follow fitness plan (15-60 mins. x 3 times per week)

Take a moment and write down your next three steps to achieve a simple goal.

1. Put the steps in order.

2. Schedule at least the first step.

3. Do the task when scheduled.

Repeat.

This method is designed to help you identify and execute simple steps. It is great for daily activities and if you want to create simple longer-term visions. The size of the step may be different, but you will follow the same principle.

How to Chunk It Down and Execute

Depending on the size of the goal you are trying to achieve, you may find it useful to break down reaching it into achievable steps. If you can't see the small steps that you need to take, use the following methods to help create your plan.

Achievable Steps

With this method, simply note down the identifiable steps to achieve a goal.

For example: I want to sell some of my belongings on eBay to save toward a holiday.

Assuming you haven't used eBay before, these could be the steps:

1. Get an eBay account

2. Learn how to create a listing (watch some videos)

3. Identify what you will sell (high-value small items are best for mailing)

4. Create the listings (photos, description, price, postage)

5. Get packing materials (boxes are available in many post offices)

6. Prepare and pack sold items

7. Mail items

The size of the steps is up to you — don't make them too small, as you will spend a lot of time identifying the steps instead of working on them. If the chunks are too big, you'll know because you will get distracted by other easier activities and not work on your goal. Subconsciously it will seem too hard, and this is when we look for immediate gratification. So if you sense yourself being affected that way, think of your goal and identify the smallest next step you can take. Then take it. This could be just opening a text message, getting into your gym clothes, walking for one minute, or taking any tiny step that will move you forward. When I'm facing tasks I don't want to do, but I know are good for me, sometimes I say to myself, for instance, that *all I have to do is switch on the computer and open the document or email*. If I still don't feel like doing it, I can stop. Inevitably, when I write that one email or do that one thing, I feel soooooo much better about myself, so remember this when you get distracted.

By the way, speaking as someone who uses eBay, I know that most people could start right now on that list and have an eBay listing up in a couple of hours.

This method of breaking down the steps is great, but when it comes to the execution, some people don't always know how to do it.

Commit Some Time

I've been in LA for about six years and have some incredible friends here. There are enough of them that I can guarantee every week there are invites to parties, openings, friends performing, dance parties, yoga sessions, or who knows what else. Those activities are on top of all the hobbies I have myself and all the house renovations my wife and I are doing. Add to that our work lives, and it's surprising we get anything done.

One way to ensure you do achieve some of your bigger goals is to set aside time weekly or daily to focus on your list. Think about each day of the week and where you could take fifty minutes to work on your goals. Schedule in a few sessions. I also highly recommend writing your goals on a Post-it and displaying it somewhere you'll see it to keep it front of mind.

There are other things you can do to create time for yourself. I often set my alarm early in the morning, so I can get up and enjoy some of the day before I start work. If you are a morning person, this is a great time to get some tasks done — even if you only give it twenty-five minutes. There may be time between when you get home and before your evening meal...so that's another twenty-five minutes, which means you're done with your goal. You'll be amazed at how much you can achieve and how good you'll feel about it by simply using a little bit of time and taking some action.

Taking the eBay example, you may choose to work on the list for three x 50-minute blocks in a week, and the task will be completed over as many periods as are required and will take far less time.

Plan the Next Block Before the Current One Ends

Whenever possible, schedule your time in advance. When we are in a reactive state, we tend not to be as productive or resourceful, so get used to planning your time, and you will start making progress more quickly. When you commit time to an activity, you are also creating space in your life for not thinking about that activity, which will help you stay more present in the other things you do.

Getting into the habit of planning your next day (tasks, lunch, exercise, calls, etc.) the day before will reap rewards in the form of your certainty and confidence.

Use Your Natural High to Keep the Momentum

As mentioned previously, dopamine is a natural drug released by our brains when we achieve something we set out to do. When you don't feel like going to the gym, getting on the treadmill or doing some weights seems like a horrible idea. However, once you get there, isn't it strange that you tend to keep going and do a full session? That's because you're feeling good about yourself for getting there, and then you feel good about doing the treadmill, so the weights don't feel so bad. This happens because you were designed this way, and life wants to reward you for acting.

Parkinson's Law

You will always have tasks to do, so never expect to have no to-do list. Parkinson's Law suggests:

If you don't fill up your time with high priority items, it will get filled with low priority items.

It's not just your time that's affected. Low-priority items can fill up energy, money, and any other resources. Notice how easy it is to follow the path of least resistance when temptation calls. Having a plan provides you with an easy alternative to temptation and helps keep you focused and on track.

When you know you have planned something, you know that you don't need to worry about it anymore; you have a sense

---

of certainty and, remember, that also helps build your confidence.

Having a basic plan can instantaneously dispel concerns. For example, this could be knowing where the fire escape is, or who to call in an emergency.

There are also disadvantages to planning—some of us like to go with the flow and take our life path as it comes. Being too organized can reduce the freedom we have. That's true, but it doesn't mean not planning anything at all. It's about achieving a balance, and I think we can agree that most of us could do with more effective planning in our lives, to get more of what we want and give more of the gift of who we are.

Remember, choosing is exercising your freedom of choice.

Find Your Inspiration

A little bugbear of mine is that I think it is socially unfair that so many of us as children were asked what we were going to be and do when we grew up. The same happened when we were coming to the end of our school careers, and for those who continued learning, again toward the end of our further education. There are thousands of types of jobs in the world that involve a massive range of similar and different skills, and asking someone to commit to an occupation can be a huge burden, especially if they aren't sure what to choose but are pressured to decide and follow through. It's great if a child has a natural affinity for a career; however, my experience is that most of us don't know what we want and don't really understand what many jobs entail, anyway. I have worked as a bacon packer, fruit picker, and fire performer, as well as a trainer in the mining, casino, healthcare, aerospace, and investment industries. I sold photocopier software, tried my hand with two network marketing companies, and taught children French. Many of those jobs were not my purpose, but all the experiences helped me clarify my path as I learned what was and wasn't my vocation.

Values can be considered the compass that guides our direction in life. Knowing and working with your values is an extremely worthwhile activity to help you feel more fulfilled because your values can assist in guiding you.

If someone values music, we find they speak about it, spend money on it, take part in it, and they're likely quite organized in that area. Similarly, if someone values cooking, we find they probably have a well-kept kitchen, sharp knives, and cooking books, and that they cook a lot. Our values are often mirrored by our behavior, but this isn't the way we are usually led to identify them.

I've attended a number of seminars where the importance of values was discussed. One perspective we covered was how having more empowering values would be beneficial in our lives. Inevitably, we attempted to identify the most honorable and positive-sounding values and insert them into our lives and, through conditioning, make them a part of us. There was some value in the process; however, it didn't feel completely natural, and I know now that was because, in my case, I chose the values consciously. The moment we get our minds involved in identifying our values, we start filtering them through our beliefs and opinions, which tarnishes reality. We may say we value learning to be a better communicator or paying off our debts, yet our behavior proves otherwise. When we truly value something, we are always looking at ways to fulfill it and are ready to put effort into having it fulfilled. People who love the gym don't hit snooze when they hear their alarm in the morning. But those of us who feel like we should be going to the gym early — but it's not in our values — will often find it much harder to get up.

When I identified my two highest values as learning and teaching, it gave me a level of certainty around what to focus my energies on in my career. In some ways, this narrowed the opportunities available to me, but that just helped me focus. I recommend repeating this exercise from time to time; however, even if you only ever do it once, I think you'll be very happy you took the time.

> *"Your actions speak so loudly I can't*
> *hear what you're saying."*
> *Ralph Waldo Emerson*

If you want to know what your values are, simply look at what your behavior displays. You can say you value health and fitness, but your food habits, the amount you exercise, and your physique are a far better indicator of your commitment to those values.

The Demartini Value Determination Process®[14] was developed by Dr. John Demartini and is a full set of simple questions that help you clearly determine your values. I highly recommend John's **Breakthrough Experience** course, where he goes into more depth and provides a full physical and metaphysical explanation of our nature as humans as you experience his method firsthand. The learnings I've gained from spending time with him exploring the nature of the universe have had some of the most impactful effects on the quality of my life.

---

[14] *Dr. John Demartini* https://drdemartini.com/

In the meantime, here's my interpretation of his questions, which I feel adds a different dimension to his work to make it easier for you.

Before you get started, make sure you can give yourself an hour to complete this process — although you may find you can do it much faster. The value of what you'll find out makes this exercise absolutely worth doing and will improve the quality of your life by giving you certainty and clarity. Going through this process is a very exciting activity. It helps support some of your current beliefs, and you may uncover personal attributes you have been repressing. You will finally be able to give yourself permission to be, do, and have those things in your life which you desire.

Why It's Useful to Know Your Values

Your values guide you in life and can help you see your purpose in a field where you can be rewarded handsomely. Your behavior demonstrates that many of the things you do every day are primarily to help you achieve more of your highest values. If you want to be rewarded more, learn how to help more people using your highest value — that's your purpose.

With the knowledge of your hierarchy of values, you will start to understand yourself better historically, as well as discover where your path forward might be. Notice now that at an unconscious level, your behavior shows you are constantly seeking out ways you can get more of your highest values fulfilled. For example, I love *learning* and *teaching* and consume a lot of information all the time. I regularly tell friends (and strangers) all about what I've learned, and the corporate job I've done for years is to train people. This feels great to me, and like I'm sharing my gift. However, converting the information into a book has been challenging for me because

100

once I put the main body together, I wasn't learning so much anymore; I wasn't getting immediate feedback for my teaching, so it was hard to get me started.

When our values are not fulfilled, we are far more reactive...

Recall a time you overreacted to someone. When you reflect on that moment, consider that it is likely your values weren't being fulfilled much at the time because we are more sensitive and react when our values tank is low. One of the side effects of being purposeful and fulfilled is that we can become far more patient and forgiving of others who are on their journey because we appreciate what it's like not to have direction.

Uncover Your Values Exercise[15]

Duration: 30-60 minutes

Materials: Grab a pen and some paper and prepare to uncover your values.

As you go through the questions, list at least 3-5 answers for each question. When you reach the end of the questions, go back through your list and circle the answers you see more than once, so don't worry about repetition. Finishing this exercise is more important than doing it perfectly. Just have fun and scribble away.

What is a Value?

A value is something you consider worthy or important such as: security, adventure, creativity, health, financial wealth,

---

[15] *The questions and ideas behind this content are from Dr. John Demartini – The Demartini Value Determination Process™. For further details and an opportunity to use his online form for this process, go to www.drdemartini.com.*

your children, helping the environment, learning about personal growth, charity, knowledge, sewing, cooking, dancing, etc.

Step One

These are the questions, and the idea is that you answer each with your top three answers. There are details explaining each question to help guide you:

1. How do you fill your primary personal or professional **space** most?

   - Technology, music, cooking tools, personal development books, clothes, crystals, craft supplies...

2. How do you spend your **time** most when you are awake?

   - Cooking, working, exercising, following politics, learning, traveling...

3. How do you spend your **energy** most, and what energizes you?

   - Listening to people, helping others, uplifting music, focusing on getting a relationship...

4. How do you spend your **money** most?

   - Restaurants, internet/phone, socializing, hobby, home...

5. Where are you most **organized** and ordered the most?

   - In the kitchen, on your phone, with your contacts, knowing where live music is...

6. Where are you most **reliable**, disciplined, and focused?

   - Meeting up with people, at work, at events, dressing well, eating healthy...

7. What do you **inwardly think** about most?

   - Getting a great relationship, being healthier, enjoying work more...

8. What do you **visualize** and then realize most?

   - Living in a certain area, buying a house, traveling overseas, creating a family...

9. What do you **internally dialogue** about most?

   - Getting healthier, building your business, starting your own business...

10. What do you **talk about most to others** in a social setting?

    - Family, vacations, building your business, things you've learned, health...

11. What **inspires** you most?

    - Amazing music, heartfelt friendships, fast cars, sports...

12. What are your most consistent and **persistent long-term goals** that are coming true?

    - Writing a book, starting a business, creating a home, learning a new skill...

13. What do you most love **learning**, reading, studying, or listening to?

    - Psychology, the environment, helping people, travel...

IMPORTANT: READ ME
Immediate Gratification and
Decoding your values

Immediate Gratification

We spend time on things that give us immediate pleasure when we are not inspired by bigger goals. For example, if you usually stay up late distracted by social media, or you enjoy having a few extra drinks which make you feel tired in the morning, it is highly unlikely you would do these things if the next day you had the most amazing vacation planned with your best friends doing your favorite things. When something is truly important to you, the time vampire of distraction loses its power, and instead, you create fuel to pursue your higher intentions. You replace satisfaction in the moment with a longer-term benefit. This may mean going to bed excitedly before your vacation, and maybe that keeps you up a bit, but you would not want to waste time on lower priority activities to ruin a special vacation for you. It is possible you'll find you spend a lot of time distracting yourself, that's fine, but look for the inspiration and the things you love to do.

Entertainment for Distraction

Entertainment can serve a range of purposes. Sometimes it allows us to unwind and relax, and other times, it is there to fill us with energy and excitement. If you notice you have items you could group into a category of *entertainment*, look deeper at their content, but be cautious whether you include it as a value. I watch lots of YouTube videos — some are educational and satisfy my desire to learn. However, other videos are purely for entertainment. I don't include the latter in my value determination. If you were a musician who watched videos for inspiration and ideas, then that would be included in the value of perhaps, *creating music* or *connection through music*.

Decoding Your Values

Remember to decode the responses you give. For instance, if you surround yourself with books, what kind of books are they, what are the topics? Spending time at work could be because you value security or family, and so you work to create that at home, or you could enjoy work because of the nature of what you do, and money is a byproduct. If you like gardening, is it because you feel connected to nature or because you like growing vegetables to cook? If you go to festivals or events, what interests you most? Is it the people you want to be around, the music, stalls, or something else?

Reflect on your answers to see if they have a deeper purpose. If someone surrounds themselves with family photos, they will likely value family, compared to a photographer who may have photos around but values the skill or the art of photography. Also, the same thing may mean different things to different people. Some people may use social media to escape, whereas others use it for their business, or to connect or share.

In this exercise, remember we're looking for the actions you take when you're not filling your time with immediate gratification.

And for simplicity and clarity, the value should be one word or a short phrase (as long as it is specific). For example: health, adventure, or connected to nature, raising a family.

The simpler you make the description of the value, the easier it will be to achieve.

Here are examples of how to decode values:

- Going to work: what do you get from work that is important to you? Do you learn how to advance your career and make more money, do you just love accountancy and get satisfaction completing somebody's books, do use the money you make to spend on your family or hobbies? Do you feel strongly about the purpose of a company and want to get the message out there? Values in these examples could be *money, contentment, family, hobbies, or perhaps the environment.*

- Shopping: what kind of items are you buying — are they to help you look good, stand out, or fit in? Are they to improve your home, activities to help you get into a relationship, organic and whole foods, music, tickets? Each provides a different value such as *beauty, creativity, creating a home, connection, health, or music.*

- Looking good: what specifically is it that you get from looking good? Is health important to you, or maybe you want to attract someone and create a family or feel companionship? Are you a creative person, and your clothing is a canvas to express yourself? As you can see, it is important to decode the answers you get to these questions. *Looking good* in this example could relate to values such as *health, family, or creativity.*

1. How do you fill your primary personal or professional space most?

Have you ever noticed that things which are not important to you get placed in piles, stored somewhere for later, discarded or deleted? By contrast, the things you feel are important are placed where you can see and access them — either at home, work, or on your desktop.

What does your life demonstrate through your physical space? When you look around your room, office, or where you spend your time, do you see photos, clothing, art, or books on relationships? Do you see items that represent nature, comfortable furniture for friends to sit on or souvenirs of favorite places you've visited? Perhaps your space is full of musical instruments, or tools for creativity or technology. Whatever you see around you is a very strong clue as to what you value most.

Also, consider your virtual space, the space on your phone, or computer. Is your memory filled with photographs of children, acoustic music, selfies, or audible tracks or apps? What is all over your Instagram feed and what is on your screensaver, your profile, and the wall photos on your online media right now? Outside of entertainment or distraction, what apps do you fill your phone with that are important to you? What's on your main screen? Look at how your space is filled and define what it means to you.

What three things fill your space?

2. How do you spend your time most when you are awake?

People always make time for things that are really important to them and run out of time for things that aren't. Even though many usually say, *I don't have time for what I really want to do*; the truth is they are too busy doing what is most important to them. What they think they want to be doing isn't really what's most important. Every day you have twenty-four hours of the raw material of life, and you always find time for things that are really important to you.

So, how do you spend your time?

My work revolves around building training materials and communicating, which are two things I love, and the money that comes from them provides me security and resources for learning, beauty, and creativity. I spend my days listening to radio programs about people, spirituality, science, and technology and then write my thoughts on how to communicate this information to people. I also love to cook, play with RC (radio-controlled) cars, and find myself watching programs online about philosophy, psychology, nature, random facts, and comedy. Learning, teaching, and being creative are three of my highest values, and I always find time for them. However, I almost never find time for opera or watching sports, which are low on my list of values. How you spend your time tells you what matters most to you.

In which three ways do you spend your time?

3. How do you spend your energy most, and what energizes you?

You always have energy for things that inspire you — the things you value most. You run out of energy for things that don't. Notice how you feel when you're preparing to go on holiday — excited and energized or tired and uninterested? Things that are low in your values drain you; things that are high in your values energize you. In fact, when you are doing something that you value highly, you have more energy at the end of the day than when you started because you're doing something you love and are inspired by. So, how do you spend your energy — and where do you get your energy? If you have something to do in the morning which inspires you, it's so much easier to get out of bed because you know it's waiting for you!

In which three ways do you spend your energy, and where do you feel energized?

4. How do you spend your money most?

You will always find money for things that are most important to you, but you never want to part with your money for things that are not important to you. Your choices about spending money tell you a great deal about what you value most. Some people notice they spend money on things they don't really want to, such as insurance or vet bills, then they'll notice that they value the health of their animals and so are prepared to spend the money. It's also important to decode your answers to all these questions, since someone who spends a lot of money on a TV or audio equipment may actually value the music or the sports programs they watch and not the technology itself — except as a *means value* where we're looking for *ends values*.

In which three ways do you spend your money?

At this point, you may be noticing some overlap: some similarities between what you fill your space with and how you spend your time, energy, and money. That is healthy and what we'd hope to see. If you find you have a wide variety of answers, look more closely at why you chose those values, and you may find an encompassing value that covers a range of ideas. I take photos of many things, scenes, and people, but the underlying value which drives my photo-taking is *beauty & creativity,* which, to me, represents one value. If two values have a lot of similarities, see if they can be grouped in a way that feels right for you. The meaning you give it is most important.

5. Where are you most organized and ordered the most?

We tend to bring order and organization to things that are important to us and to allow chaos and disorder in things that are low in our values. Assess where you have the greatest order and organization in your life, and you'll have a good sense of what matters most to you.

In my case, I am very organized in my online storage, which enables me to easily access the documents, photos, and apps— which help me learn and teach. When it comes to cooking, I also know where all my ingredients and cookware are. This helps me see that my values involve learning, teaching, and creativity (in food and photography).

In which three areas are you most organized?

6. Where are you most reliable, disciplined, and focused?

You never have to be reminded from the outside to do the things you value the most. You are inspired from within to do those things, and so you do them. Look at the activities, relationships, conference calls, and goals where you are disciplined, reliable, and focused. These are areas where you already actively self-start and look for opportunities.

In which three activities and areas are you most reliable, disciplined, and focused?

7. What do you inwardly think about most?

I'm not talking about the negative self-thought or what distracts you. I'm not talking about the fantasies or the "shoulds." I'm talking about your most common thoughts concerning how you want your life to be. You're looking for evidence of them actually coming to fruition, even if it is over time. For me, this includes designing and delivering my courses, writing my book, and inspiring people.

What are your three most dominant thoughts?

8. What do you visualize and then realize most?

Again, I'm not talking about fantasies. I'm asking what you visualize for your life that is slowly but surely coming true. In my case, I **visualize delivering my courses and creating environments where these lessons can be learned and implemented.** That is what I visualize. And that is what I am realizing. So, what are you visualizing and realizing?

What are the three ways in which you visualize your life?

9. What do you internally dialogue about most?

What do you keep talking to yourself about? I'm not referring to negative self-talk or self-aggrandizement. I want you to think of your preoccupation with what you desire most — the intentions that seem to be coming true and showing some fruits.

What are the three things you talk to yourself about most?

10. What do you talk about most to others in a social setting?

Now, these are habits that you'll probably notice in other people as well as in yourself. What are the topics that you keep wanting to bring into the conversation that nobody has to remind you to talk about? What subjects turn you into an instant extrovert? Whether your baseline personality is extrovert or introvert, you've probably noticed there are topics that immediately bring you to life — they start you talking. Other subjects turn you into an introvert with nothing to say, or they make you want to change the subject. You can use this same insight to analyze other people's values. If you're talking to somebody and they ask about your kids, that means *their* kids are important to them. If they say, "How's business?" they value business. If they ask, "Are you seeing anyone new?" then, relationships matter to them. Topics that attract you are a key to what you value.

What are the three top things that you speak to others about in social settings?

11. What inspires you most?

What inspires you now? What has inspired you in the past? What is common to the people who inspire you? When you get a tear in your eye at somebody's performance, why does that happen to you; what does it mean? When things happen that bring a tear to your eye, this is often an indication that you are inspired by something. Figuring out what inspires you most reveals what you value most.

What are the three things that inspire you the most?

12. What are your most consistent and persistent long-term goals that are coming true?

What long-term goals of yours are frequently in your mind? Is there anything you've been thinking or talking about for a while that you are seeing come to fruition? Again, it is important that this is not a pipe dream or an injected goal — your behavior will show frequent signs of the goals which are truly important to you.

My book falls into this category. There were times my focus went elsewhere, and I made slow progress, but over time I could see it coming together. Your goals could be a skill, a car, a home, a piece of art or furniture you've wanted to create, a vacation...

What are your three most consistent and persistent long-term goals?

13. What do you most love learning, reading, studying, or listening to?

What are the top three common topics you most love learning or reading about? What three topics can you stay focused on, and do you love learning about without distraction? This could be time you spend online reading or listening to audios. If you look at your video history, are there things you watch consistently to learn about?

What are the three things you love to learn and read about?

Step Two

1.   For each question where you have more than three answers, review them, and identify the top three. As mentioned, decode your answers to identify what the

113

thing or idea represents to you and group like values into the same value.

- For example, if art came up a lot in your list, the value of art is a very broad topic. It could be that underlying the art, in the value, may be beauty (it's about the look), creativity (perhaps you made it), or financial wealth (you may be an art investor).

- For me, beauty & creativity are so closely linked that they represent the expression of one value. I really enjoy photography — especially of things I feel are beautiful. But I also love editing images, creating videos, and using multimedia to show or share my art. Trust your intuition if you are not sure of a value's position to see if it's in your top three. If you need to, compare it to another value and decide what you'd prefer if you could only have 100 percent of one and none of the other. This helps determine the hierarchy.

2. Once you've identified three answers for each of the thirteen questions, you'll see that among your thirty-nine answers is a certain amount of repetition.

3. **TIP:** Fine-tune anything for clarity — again look for similar items that are coming up as two separate values when underlying them may be the same thing or values which are at too high a level such as food, sports, learning. These could easily decode to cooking food, physical fitness, or learning about investing.

4. Circle the answer that comes up most frequently, and the second most frequently, etc. This will show you your hierarchy of values.

5. Keep in mind you may be expressing the same kind of value in different ways. For example, you might enjoy socializing but have written down *spending time socializing at work, having a drink with friends,* and *spending money going out to restaurants with friends.* But if you look closely, the value could be socializing, connecting with a particular person, or something else.

6. Rewrite your values in order and see if they feel correct. When you read the first three, they should feel very natural because this is what your behavior displays. If any don't feel quite right yet, it's worth it to analyze them more closely to see if an underlying value is present.

7. Knowing your values provides a level of certainty in yourself and an ability to communicate with others. I remember the feeling I had when I first saw that my two highest values were learning and teaching. That made so much sense to me and helped me realize where I should focus my energies in my work and life.

What Is Your Purpose?

Why are we here? What are we supposed to do? These are questions to which we all want answers.

Although I can't tell you your answers, I can show you how to act on purpose, and I'll give you some specific guidance based on wisdom and values. As a bonus, I'll share the three magic words to explain how to act on your purpose if you're still unsure of your way of expressing it.

Following the completion of the previous exercise, you'll notice you spend most of your energy achieving your highest value. The Greeks called this your *telos*, and *teleology*[16] is the study of your highest value. When you fulfill your telos, you will have the highest level of alignment with who you are. A bottle cap can be used for many creative and productive purposes; however, it shows its strongest attributes when used to hold back immense pressure in a soda bottle. When we act in alignment with our highest value, we are living on purpose. Like a yacht, when the wind catches its sail, we feel aligned, directed, certain, and powerful.

Exercise: How can you get rewarded for what you love to do?

This exercise is designed to create possibility around identifying the kinds of ways you could get rewarded for following your purpose. I believe the universe wants you to be handsomely rewarded in love and money for living your purpose, and this exercise is designed to help fulfill that. Please approach it with curiosity and a sense of fun. The seed of a single idea you come up with could grow a whole new world for you in time. This uses a visual representation like a mind map to help you make new connections between your values and what you can do for work.

The answers are just for you, so don't hold back!

Steps:

1. Grab a fresh piece of paper. You may want some notepaper handy, too.

2. Write down your highest value from the previous exercise in the middle of the page and draw a circle

---

[16] *https://en.wikipedia.org/wiki/Teleology*

around it. If you're not sure which is your highest, just choose one that feels right.

3. Next, write down at least four keywords representing different things you love. These could be activities, items or hobbies which make you really happy, anything. Ideally, space them out evenly around the first circle. Draw a circle around each of the keywords.

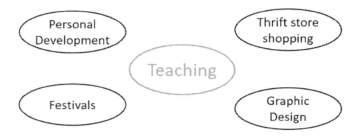

4. On the next level out, note three ideas, jobs, ways to make money, or occupations where you could fulfill your highest value using the things you love. Don't

worry about the detail of the ideas, how much money you could make at this point, or whether it is even realistic. Just note down ideas that will provide stepping stones later for what you're trying to achieve.

1. Write a blog or book on topics I love to help others feel inspired
2. Become a coach in the areas I feel confident
3. Create other online products teaching the skills I love.

1. Teach how to make money selling what I find thrift shopping
2. Teach how to use thrift stores to save money on home upgrades
3. Create a blog to educate about markets and thrift stores.

1. Teach my personal development tools at festivals
2. Teach how to take great festival photos at a festival
3. Teach about festival preparation tips and tricks.

1. Teach simple graphic design for home users
2. Teach how to make logos and edit photos for websites
3. Use Fiverr, Upwork or other online resources to sell my skills.

At this point, you may already have come up with some new ideas to get you thinking and remember there is a huge market on the internet for people wanting to learn what you know and productizing your information into courses, podcasts, videos, and products is always an option. I really like Amy Schmittauer's channel Savvy Sexy Social to learn about how to become a vlogger (video blogger).

5. Add some ideas: I highly recommend explaining this exercise to a friend without telling them the ideas you've written and asking them how they think you

could make money using your value and your area of interest.

- For example, "How do you think I could make money using graphic design and teaching?" You may be surprised at the ideas you get. Add these to your paper.

6. Leverage with Google: To add even more ideas to your page, search online for: "How to make money from…" and use some of your keywords. Try something like:

- "How to make money from graphic design," or "How to make money at festivals."

- Once complete, you will have a list of ideas, which will probably excite you as you read them, and hopefully, you can already see some new possibilities.

7. Review and refine: Rewrite and order your list, removing anything which doesn't feel right. Talk to people about the ideas that make you most excited. I encourage you to connect with people who know the industries because, unlike the internet, people tend to make interesting connections, and technology does not. My wife works for a mobile zoo, and friends have had the opportunity to help out for a day, taking chickens, ferrets, goats, pythons, tarantulas, chinchillas, and more to parties — all because they spoke to her about it. This would be a great way for someone interested in animals to explore whether they'd like working with them.

8. **Call for a catchup:** Over the next week, research your areas of interest and ask questions of people who know about them. If done with the right intention and approach, it is quite appropriate to call someone doing a job you'd like to do and ask if they'd be free for five minutes (either then or at a later time, when you can call back) to answer a handful of questions about their job and what it is like because you're thinking about working in that field. Make sure you prepare around five open-ended questions you want to know answers to, and hopefully, the conversation will provide new insights and possibly even a connection.

The idea of this exercise is to create new, unexpected possibilities and not necessarily give you the exact answer — this is a step on the path. I have found that being unconventionally creative can help with uncovering what is important to us so we may pursue it, whilst enjoying the process of life even more.

Maybe you just want a Job: If you are not an entrepreneur, and would rather work for someone else, you can use the same format of questioning to help you identify the kind of jobs you'd most like to do. Once you get clarity on that, use Google to find the kinds of companies that have the kinds of roles in the areas which appeal to you and learn about them. Also, reach out to their HR departments to ask if they have people you can talk to about their jobs in the departments which interest you. With the right attitude, people are very willing to help.

For example, on a call to HR if someone were starting to research a new career, I might say:

"Hi ...., I hope you can *help me*. My name is... and I'm interested in becoming a graphic designer. I've been doing some research, and I'd like to know *if it would be possible* for you to find someone who would be *open* to have a chat with me who knows this area. I have prepared a few questions, and I could send them to you in advance."

I'm not saying this text is guaranteed to work, but I hope you sense the way I'm approaching the call. **Note**: The words in *italics* are great to include as people find them safe and generally respond well to them subconsciously.

In my experience, people don't usually find their purpose in a lightning bolt or an "aha" moment. We are more likely to stop one day and realize we've been living our purpose without realizing it. Use these new insights about yourself to help you focus your attention and either start taking steps toward what is important to you or change how you see your current situation to make the most of it.

See It the Same, but Different

At times in my life, I've lived and worked away from home for months on end, which I could easily have seen as a chore. All that packing up, getting up early, flying for hours, etc. However, I chose to see it as an adventure and would enjoy exploring the towns and meeting new people. Once, I found gem fields near where I worked and would fossick for sapphires and zircons during my time off (I actually used the stones I found for my wife's wedding ring!). I joined a local poker tournament, and in another town of a few hundred people, I enjoyed opera and comedy at a local variety show. Alternatively, if I was on a mining camp in one of the most remote places in the world such as Newman in Western

Australia with few people I knew and not much to do, I would go on walks, take photos and use the opportunity to keep fit by taking runs before sunset. Sometimes you won't want to or be able to change your situation. But a subtle change in your perception can turn a chore into a charm. Thanks to this perspective, I had such a good time away from home, and some of my photography and stories even made it into the *Australian National Press*.

> *"There is a direct relationship between what you do and how much it serves your highest values."*

Are They Stumbling Blocks or Building Blocks?

All the new ideas and information I've shared with you may make you feel overwhelmed. Please remember that this is a summary of a range of ideas I've learned and practiced over the years. It would be crazy to think you could assimilate it all immediately.

I heard of an excellent remedy for overwhelm (and you may have heard this before…). If ever you feel like you don't know what to do, think of one thing you want, then break it down into steps, prioritize the steps, and take the first one. I've tried to make this easier for you by including the Inspiring Menus section in the back of the book. You may want to skip ahead now and take a glance to see how easy it can be to learn and practice what I've shared.

Chapter 6: Communication

A number of years ago, I ended up stuck on a street in Saigon in the early hours of the morning with no apparent way to get into the guesthouse where I was staying. The door had been chained and padlocked. The friend I was with had already disappeared into his hostel a street away and was nowhere to be seen. This was before smartphones, so at 3 am I was literally a street person, with no money and nobody to call. (Incidentally, I had dropped my remaining Vietnamese dong [their currency] when I took something out of my pocket on the way home, just before a bunch of street kids wanted to arm wrestle for money, but that's a story for another day.)

I tried talking to a few people, but they didn't speak English, and my Vietnamese is very limited. I noticed an older lady who was tending a little street café and thought I'd at least try and get a cup of tea whilst I waited for the next few hours for someone to open the guesthouse door for me. The woman didn't respond well to our confusing communication, so I found a spot and lie down on the ground with my head on a concrete step as a pillow to get try to get some sleep; the thought of cockroaches crawling in my mouth quickly dispelled that fantasy, however.

Then I remembered something subtle, yet of vital importance. Vietnam was part of French Indochina up until 1954. The café woman was past middle age, so I decided to change my communication strategy — I sidled back up to the woman and said, "Est-ce que vous parlez Français?" Translated to mean, "Do you speak French?"

Within seconds, a beautiful old smile spread across her face, and she confirmed that she spoke French. Moments later, we were chatting away, and I learned about her life growing up in

Vietnam during the wars, as well as all about her family. I even scored a free cup of tea whilst I waited for morning.

It may seem unusual to many people to speak a European language to an Asian person and expect them to understand; however, that tiny change in my communication technique revolutionized the whole experience for us both, creating a win/win situation. Remember, even if what you're saying makes sense to you, sometimes your words sound like a foreign language to others. If you reflect a moment, you'll see it's clear that we do not all communicate using the same dialect, even when we're speaking the same language!

Never Underestimate the Value of Learning a Foreign Language

There they were, running, jumping, playing, and having so much fun. These baby mice were so excited about seeing the world. Their mother watched caringly, so they didn't get into too much trouble. Then, one of them froze, and out of the corner of her eye, the mother saw the face of the tomcat. Eyes like saucers, lips dripping saliva, and if that cat could say one thing, it would have said, "Dinnertime." Immediately, the mother dived between her babies and the cat, looked it dead in the eyes, and said, "Woof, woof, wooooof! Wooof, woof!" The cat was so shocked and confused; it ran away! Sensing the calm had returned to the area, the mother turned to her babies, and calmly said, "Never underestimate the value of learning a foreign language."

Instead of theory, I'll be covering practical tools you can use today.

Given the importance of communication, it surprises me that more emphasis isn't placed on educating people on this topic in our schooling system. Great communication leads to flow, growth, and ease, which allows us to move through the world smoothly, achieving more of what we want.

I appreciate the Nero-linguistic Programming (NLP) model of communication, which identifies how we delete, distort and generalize information we experience, and then put it through the filters of our values, beliefs, opinions, language, metaprograms,[17] and decisions. We then mix that with our physiology to create an internal representation, kind of like the movie we're projecting onto our screen, and this leads to our behavior. However, as I stated, I do not intend to go into the theory behind communication and instead will focus on specific phrases or sayings I've found helpful and which you can use to improve your ability to communicate and ask for what you want.

My wife has identified that I have an uncanny willingness and ability to ask for things and often get what I want... She says my ability to *ask effectively* seems to give me an advantage in moving through life. I'm, therefore, going to share some of the ideas which help me ask effectively, so you can, too.

---

[17] *A metaprogram is a non-hierarchical value. For example, one metaprogram is called the Direction Filter — some people prefer to move toward pleasure and others to move away from pain. Otherwise said, some people go on vacation for an adventure and some to get away from work. This is a kind of value, but it has no greater importance than other values.*

What Is Communication, Really?

The word *communication*[18] comes from the Latin *communicare — to share*. When we communicate, we share information. The Latin definition is a HUGE clue to the breadth of communication available to us if we pay it attention. However, most people focus on words only when they consider this topic. Although important, we'll also touch on how information is being shared with us from other sources in our lives, such as technology; I'm sure you understand that the way we communicate with computers, can have a big impact on what we achieve.

Humans are broadcast and reception machines. We take in information through our five senses, and as we respond, we broadcast our reaction for others to receive and process. For example, if you were to touch something hot and jump back, your physical response would communicate to anyone watching that the surface you touched was hot.

It is easy to limit thinking about communication to meaning *spoken* or *written language* between people, but that is the tip of the iceberg of the communication happening around you right now. Whether it's the color of the sky, or the smell of fresh bread as you walk past a bakery, information is constantly being communicated to you. This can be in the form of *words* or *tonality,* but you can also perceive it through *color*, *shape*, *weight*, *texture*, *smell,* or *any other attribute* you're able to take in through your senses.

---

[18] *https://www.lexico.com/en/definition/communicate*

The Power of Asking

As you may have gathered from my life story, I've had a very unusual journey. I've enjoyed great success in a range of important areas (such as work, health, and relationships) and am confident at asking for what I need in such a way that it makes others want to help.

I've found that asking usually goes hand in hand with confidence, and I've become more confident over time from asking in many different situations, from boardrooms to coal mines, from world capitals to almost uninhabited islands. In addition, I'm willing to ask and am confident I can deal with rejection. A small sample of the value of my achievements include:

- Meeting and marrying an incredible woman.

- Being given half a company to run when I took a job as a director.

- Gaining a sixty percent pay raise in the same field by asking for it.

- Getting my bank to lower my interest rate substantially because I said I couldn't afford to pay them.

- Convincing a foreign bank to write off over £10,000 debt for a friend who had cancer.

- Using Jedi mind tricks to get into France without a passport.

Why Asking?

I've found that my ability to ask has had a huge impact on the quality of my life (and the lives of the people around me). This skill includes my ability to listen to the response and take any additional steps to achieve the outcome I desire. Sometimes, people would consider such tools a little manipulative; however, I feel that the intention behind the use of any of these strategies is more important than the tool itself. If I help someone get something they want, it is part of the gift of life to be able to help them. That's the intention I bring to using what I'm sharing here.

Tony Robbins said that "The quality of your life is the quality of the questions you ask."

Some Unexpected Etymology

Ions-on-a-quest = quest-ions

Consider a positive and negative ion spinning around each other, trying to get into balance because of their different charges. Both of them are ions on a quest to get into balance. They are quest-ions.

Questions have the same purpose. When you are missing information, you ask a question to get that information. When you obtain that information, the question will no longer exist for you as you have an answer.

In-formation

Your question creates an answer filled with information. That information in your mind can grow into an idea. For that idea to take form, you will use information. Thanks to the alignment of question and answer, the *ideas in formation*, provide the *information* required to give the thought form.

I agree with that wholeheartedly and add this caveat: the questions you ask yourself AND the questions you ask of others.

What Is Asking?

When you ask a question, you are trying to reveal the unknown. This could be information, an idea, permission, or anything you don't currently have. From an energetic perspective, Asking achieves some amazing things:

- It gives the opportunity for someone to give

- It gives the opportunity to practice boundaries and say no

- It gives the opportunity to receive or learn through feedback what you need to change in your strategy — if you want this person to help

- It creates flow when one gives and receives, and fulfillment in life happens during flow

In addition, it is helpful because:

- It lets others, you, and the universe know what is important to you in that moment

- It helps you focus

- It forces you to be clear — clarity leads to power, so it makes you more powerful

- It creates the possibility of more resources and options for you

- It boosts your experience and, as a result, your confidence grows

- It gets other people talking and can put them at ease

Once you have an answer, you also need to know how to communicate to maintain and then determine the next course of action. Learning how to *ask effectively* and navigate conversations well makes a huge impact in life. We'll also cover how to deal with negative responses, should they occur.

"If you don't ask, the answer is always No."
Nora Roberts

How to Ask Effectively

To ask for something, you need to clearly know what you want. It is also very important to know the kinds of things the person you're asking wants, too. There could be a financial exchange, but often it is just the goodwill we generate when we give that we're happy to receive. We all desire specific human needs, such as to be loved and appreciated for who we are, as well as we want particular things based on our personalities and values. If you can fulfill the needs of the person you're asking, the chances of them fulfilling your needs increases dramatically.

"Asking effectively ensures
both parties grow as a result."

If you ask solely with the intention of getting more without giving anything (not even gratitude), then although at times this can work, it is not sustainable. At some point, people are going to stop giving to someone who sucks them dry of their time, energy, or money. By the way, the best way to find out what someone wants is to ask them. (*What could I do for you, so you would be willing to do this for me?*) Second to that, try to decode what people value and if you provide that, they'll be very happy to help. People like people like themselves or how they'd like to be. Pay attention to topics of conversation and other hints about someone else's values and consider researching values in NLP or through Dr. John Demartini for more information.

Fair Exchange When Asking or Giving

When we ask for something, we give someone else the opportunity to give. When we find a way to create a transaction of fair exchange whereby both parties give and receive fairly, then the chances of the transaction happening are greatly increased. In other words, you both achieve that which you're asking.

My photographer friend in Perth needed help painting his new studios. I was happy to support him and had always wanted to learn more about professional photography, so I offered to help. As a result of our conversations, I learned about the industry, and not long after, he even asked me to do a photoshoot for him. We didn't speak specifically about what I'd get in return for helping, but I was happy to give of my time as a gift. I knew I could also ask some questions. I felt that the few hours of my time were amply covered by the knowledge and experience I received. Although that wasn't specifically offered, I took control of the outcome by asking questions and therefore achieved what I wanted.

When we give of our time or energy, we feel best if we achieve a level of *fair exchange* in return. For example, you will feel better if the pay you get for your job equates in your mind to what you feel you deserve for doing it and the effort you put into it. Meaning there is an approximate balance between what we give and what we receive. Please remember this is feeling-oriented and not an exact science. The returns of giving can come in any form: money, support, a thank you, a spiritual connection, gratitude, the knowledge we helped someone, or anything else you value. We are always looking for how we can be rewarded based on our own values, so be aware that other people will not necessarily want the same rewards as you.

Giving and Being Taken Advantage Of

A lot of us love to give when we can, and we feel good about it. Before going further, I want to draw a distinction between *giving* and *being taken advantage of*.

- **Giving**: Both parties are neutral or happy about the exchange.

- **Being taken advantage of**: You feel you are losing out, and this is benefiting others in a way that's more than you're comfortable with.

Being Taken Advantage Of

When we feel we're being taken advantage of, fair exchange is not happening.

If you feel you are being taken advantage of in an area of your life, this is a mechanism from the universe designed to help you practice identifying and speaking your boundaries. In those moments, ask yourself, *what do I want instead?* And take action toward it. It could be you realize that the next time you're asked for more than you're willing to give, you need to say something different, or you may need to speak up in that moment and respect yourself, even though someone else is going to be disappointed. From my experience, clarifying what we need when we know the other person is going to be disappointed is never as bad as we think it's going to be. As humans, we're quite resourceful, and sometimes letting someone down is a much bigger gift than following through half-heartedly. They'll have to practice their resourcefulness and potentially find someone who will be much happier to help. Sometimes, better things come out of it, especially if you believe in the concept of *flow*. The key here, and the gift you can give to respect yourself and others, is to communicate the change of plan *with a sense of urgency*. Don't wait too long or until the last minute; make sure you inform them personally. If you can't tell them in person, I highly recommend a phone call or, at minimum, a voice and text message.

We speak up and then feel bad about it!

I've also noticed that sometimes when we speak up and ask for what we want instead, and the other person is agreeable to our request, we feel guilty and backpedal on the inconvenience of what they were asking for. This is just the energetic play between the two of you, and the best thing to do is just *say thank you and then stay quiet*. This may sound simple, but it can be quite challenging in the moment, although it often works out best for everyone.

Martyrs

Martyrs are the next level givers. They give everything…literally. The people known as martyrs in history were those who usually laid down their lives for a cause. We are more useful alive and thriving, so martyr-like behavior in daily life is not something to be encouraged.

People who consistently give to their detriment are illustrating that they don't value themselves as much as they could. Energetically they are saying that who or whatever it is they are giving to is more important than themselves. I'm not saying people can't have these beliefs; however, it is important to be aware of their implications and that giving to our detriment consistently can lead to problems.

If you feel this way, it is time to clarify and communicate your boundaries. We all want to be loved and appreciated for who we are, and our boundaries are part of who we are. If you feel that you keep giving to your detriment and it's really taking a toll on you, it's possible you feel you are in a very charged situation and perhaps don't see another choice. As mentioned in the Comfort Zone section, begin challenging yourself in areas outside of the charged topic and improving other abilities. Over time, you'll build the skills and muscles to speak up about your boundaries. Practicing the ideas in this book, exercising more, learning about helpful topics through videos, or making new friends are all ways we can expand our comfort zones, so we're open to overcoming some of the challenges we previously considered insurmountable.

I've been thrown into so many random situations and succeeded, I know it's possible for others to achieve more, even though initially it can be tough. Some of the random things I've overcome I've already mentioned and the list continues: I became manager of a 13th-century hotel near Cambridge in my late teens; I ran a cocktail bar in Hong Kong when I was in my twenties; I've taught some difficult children in a school in Hawaii and helped run a mobile zoo — none of these endeavors I was particularly expecting or prepared for, but I used the skills in this book to help achieve them!

Get Clarity on What You Want and What You Can Give

Not including financial and physical items, we are always able to give praise, respect, gratitude, thanks, support, and similar behaviors. Whenever you ask for something, keep gratitude in your heart and communicate it when you can (using words and actions). Most of the time, when I ask for something (in the context of this book), there is no physical exchange. As I ask, I flow these positive energies to the person and often share new information or a fun connection. I'm very sure they feel it, and the results I have received support this assumption.

Access Questions & Statements (AQS)

In the following section, I'll cover a range of phrases and questions I've picked up over the years, which I have found invaluable in conversation. They're split into **Opening, Maintaining,** and **Closing** a conversation as well as dealing with objections and interruptions. These can help very much with communication and asking for what you want. You can, however, use them anywhere they are appropriate in a conversation. Historically I have often found communication discussed as a concept with great ideas of how to communicate; however, I wanted magic words I could just say and get results. As a result, I provide the exact words and phrases to you as well as tell you how to apply them so you can start using these tools immediately.

Within the field of questions, there are those referred to as **Open** and **Closed** questions. Closed questions have single or short answers, whereas open questions require the listener to expand. A closed question would be, "Did you have fun at the party?" and an open question would be, "How did you feel about the party?" When you are trying to get someone to open up, use more open-ended questions; the inverse works if you ask closed questions as they have the effect of limiting the person responding with their answers, and it makes them talk less.

Opening a Conversation

In this section, the questions or phrases used are designed to help put your audience into a resourceful and open state, meaning that they are willing to hear what you have to say and interact with you. From there, if you choose to, you can ask for what you want more easily and have a greater chance of success.

I suggest noting these phrases down and refreshing yourself with them frequently for a few weeks until they become second nature. Then you'll have a tool kit always at the ready to connect with new people.

Can I have your opinion...?

People love to share their opinions, so when starting a conversation, ask for their opinion about any topic. A café is a great place to practice this, or you can use the following anywhere you're standing in line with strangers.

When asking for someone's opinion, consider the following for greatest success:

- Choose a subject that is either topical, in the vicinity, or about which you are passionate. Examples of questions you can ask in a café could include:

Ask: Could I get your opinion on something?

Pause a moment and then say something like:

- *Is it a smoothie or hot drink day?*

- *Do you think the special of the day is a tasty choice?*

- *Do you think this hat suits me?*

- *Do you think that croissant or that sandwich is tastier?*

- *That thing that happened on the news—do you think it is happening now more than last year?*

- OR ask whatever question you — ideally — have an interest in knowing the answer to.

Remember, you are doing this to simply open the conversation.

I'm so excitable, myself, that I'll randomly chat with people in lines about any of my recent adventures or hobbies and ask their opinions about things I show them on my phone. (Remember that if you choose to display something on your phone, make sure it is ready to show before you start the conversation to avoid any awkwardness involved in making people wait while you scroll to find it on your phone.) Sometimes, this turns into an amazing conversation and a new connection and, occasionally, people just nod and look at me strangely, so I thank them and leave the conversation. Being willing to fail to connect with people has built my confidence and personality, and the benefits in my quality of life are worth it.

Would you *help me* with something?

I used to live in a small duplex on Queen Street in the heart of Auckland, New Zealand. The entrance off the main street was a doorway between a key cutting shop and a Korean takeaway. One day I tried an experiment where I handed small squares of bubble wrap to a group of friends who were entering our place without saying a word — I just put it in their hands. I watched to see what they did as they walked up the stairs and, as you'd expect, everyone started popping it.

Similarly, people like helping other people...well, they certainly like hearing the request first to determine if they will help.

When you ask for help, you're metaphorically handing them a piece of bubble wrap, and you know they're going to at least hear what you have to say next. This is the key. The natural reaction of people being open to hearing what you're about to say is seeded with asking for help.

Depending on your level of skill, you can say almost anything because the person you're talking to is now in an open state. If you're new to using this phrase, as previously mentioned, ask a topical question about something either in the vicinity, something newsworthy, or something you're keenly interested in. Enthusiasm is communicated when you talk about things you're interested in, so keep that in mind when you choose a request.

Ask: Could you help me with something? Context: At a market

Pause a moment and then ask something like:

- *I'm trying to find a stall that sells...*

- *I'm looking for a gift for a friend who is going to be twenty-five. Do you have any suggestions?*

- *I'm going to a party and need to get something 70's style. Do you have any ideas?*

- *I'm not sure what to have for dinner tonight. Can you recommend anything?*

Remember, at this stage, you're only trying to help the other person as if they're in an open state to connect with you and chat. How you evolve the conversation after you're both open is covered in the **Maintaining a Conversation** section.

The majority of the time, people want to feel like they're open and understanding. Societally, there is a pressure to go with the flow and not against it, so if asked a question, many people would rather be able to say *yes* and feel good about it, than *no* and feel good. When you draw on these two attributes, you can use this phrase as a soft way to let someone feel in control. You're also opening them up to conversation. In addition, the word *idea* has unconscious associations to something positive. And we all like to like a new idea — it seems fresh.

Ask: Are you open to the idea...?

- *...of catching up sometime?*

- *...of going for a hike this weekend?*

- *...of going for a coffee or juice at lunchtime?*

If you know the person well, this is also a good way to open new topics of conversation gently, especially if the topic may be sensitive. You can raise it in a non-confrontational way to start the conversation.

Ask: Are you open to the idea...?

- *...of visiting my family for Christmas?*

- *...of getting a pet snake?*

- *...of moving to Australia?*

How to Give Quality Compliments

Mark Twain said: **"I can live for two months on a good compliment."**

Compliments are a wonderful way to connect with people and give a gift. They help share your appreciation and create a bond.

The problem with compliments, though, is that they often create a natural reaction from the receiver, which can lead to awkwardness in being appreciated in that way. This feeling will generally close people to communicating. There are two things to remember about compliments to help them be better received and create flow: **Step 1: Avoid complimenting the obvious** and **Step 2: Ask a question at the end**.

Step 1: Avoid complimenting something too obvious

Please feel free to compliment anything you appreciate in someone. What I've noticed, however, is that if someone hears the same thing repeatedly, they can respond automatically, and if you want to be noticed, it's valuable to be a little different. Use any special knowledge you have to see different attributes in a person that you can compliment them on.

I was explaining this idea to a friend one night whilst in a bar in Melbourne, Australia. I told him that if you gave compliments on less noticeable traits, the receiver would be even more appreciative. I will prefix this experiment by saying that I spoke in a gray area, meaning that I did feel appreciation for this person but not specifically and necessarily in this way, and wanted to illustrate the point to my friend about complimenting.

I asked him to select someone for me to go and talk to. He pointed to a girl standing at the bar ordering a drink. The moment I saw her, I noticed she wore a skirt that ended above her knees, so the backs of her knees were visible. I took a moment to appreciate them and then approached her to start a conversation.

"I hope you don't mind me saying, but I saw you at the bar, and I have this thing about the backs of people's knees, and yours are beautiful. Yeah, I know that's a bit weird, but I couldn't help saying something."

She looked a bit shocked and surprised but then smiled coyly as she twisted to try and see them (she couldn't).

"Are you out for a special occasion tonight, or is it just after-work drinks?" (It's always important to ask a question.)

We continued chatting for a moment, and I shared a random fact I'd heard that, in other languages, they have a word for that area — like knee-pit-but we don't have that in English. I then let the conversation close and returned to my friend, mission successful.

I'm not recommending being inauthentic in your compliments, and it's far easier to talk about something you do appreciate in others but be playful. You can always see traits in others, either physically or in their personality, which you can compliment. For example, "You have a really positive energy about you," or "I really like the way you laugh when you're excited."

On the other hand, if someone really does have something obvious you like, of course, you can compliment that aspect. If delivered well, the compliment will frequently be well-received.

Finally, on this point, if you **compliment an action** a person is performing, this prevents them from being able to deflect the compliment.

- You're listening very intently, and that feels very comforting.

- I appreciate the way you choose your fashion; it's stylish.

To identify action compliments, consider slotting an "ing" word into the phrase such as, *"I like the way you're watching, preparing, organizing, connecting, learning..."*

Step 2: Ask a question

The second part of complimenting is asking a question at the end. This gives the benefit of letting the person receive the compliment but doesn't leave the conversation open without direction. Usually, it is effective to ask about something relating to whatever you're complimenting, such as:

- Those are stylish glasses, where did you get them?

- I love the way you always ask questions. What areas are you interested in yourself?

- I've seen your feed on Instagram, and it is awesome. Where did you take all those tropical photos?

You can ask indirectly related questions, but they should be relevant. In my early career, I worked for a management consultancy firm in London, and one day, when I was working remotely in Yorkshire, I tried to start a conversation with the other, older consultants. I had heard them talking about golf, so I asked them if they played. One consultant responded yes they did and then asked if I did, which I didn't, so the conversation dried up on the spot in an awkward silence.

As you get more confident and experienced, you can ask more unrelated questions. But the way you maintain the conversation will be more challenging. Initially, I recommend only asking related questions so as not to confuse people.

Deflecting and Receiving Compliments

Often, when the receiver of the compliment hears what you say, they'll deflect the response and put themselves down. In my opinion, this is due to the inescapable balance taking place in the universe at all times: you just raised the person up energetically, and if they aren't skilled at receiving a compliment, they'll put themselves down to balance the equation. The fact is that both things were happening at the same time, but when you put your focus on one side, your subconscious mind immediately finds the balance to contextualize what has been said. **Learning to receive compliments is an easy and healthy thing to do: Simply say thank you and then remain quiet. Or put the compliment in your back pocket for when you need it later.**

Now that you are aware of this information, and if you really care about the person you are complimenting, give them the gift of a question at the end of your compliment. This will guide their attention and help prevent them from putting themselves down. It also has the tendency to open conversations.

How to Receive a Compliment

If you are given a compliment, and that awkward silence happens, say thank you as mentioned previously and, if you choose to, a simple reciprocation of a compliment is socially appreciated. Alternatively, you can expand on whatever they complimented and tell them more, or I find the following phrase leaves a pleasant feeling without further conversation required:

Thank you, that's a lovely thing to say.

If you don't often give compliments, expand your comfort zone by aiming to give five authentic compliments a day for a week. Feel free to do this with family and friends but also try and compliment strangers or even yourself! Perhaps a salesclerk, receptionist, or maybe someone in a restaurant.

I made a point of getting to know our postman and sharing a bit of myself and my hobbies with him, so he'd understand all the deliveries. I thanked him for the way he put parcels on our step, even though he could, in theory, leave them near the mailbox by the gate. I also appreciate so much what our garbage collection company does. It's amazing to think, but if they went on strike for a couple of weeks in any city, it's likely the place would grind to a halt and become rat-infested. I often wave or smile to the guys if I see them in the morning on our street because I appreciate the importance of what they do. This isn't directly a compliment, but the intention behind it is to say, *thank you for what you do.* It helps create good feelings, even without speaking. I know of at least one time that they have moved our bins when they weren't properly out for collection, which is more than is required of them.

Three Top Questions on Their Mind...

Years ago, I came across Robert Kiyosaki's book, *Rich Dad, Poor Dad*, and one of the things I took away was the importance of learning about sales because selling is something we all do every day. Until that point, I had disliked salespeople, and the word *sales* made me think about *being sold to*, which felt like manipulation. I now realize this is an outdated description of sales. I feel the new paradigm of sales is:

Helping someone get something they want.

With that in mind, I learned about the three top questions in anyone's mind when they hear someone selling something. (This could be a product or service, or simply an idea, such as *do you want to go to the beach this weekend? It's going to be a great day*. The idea of going to the beach is being *sold* to the person, and if they buy it, they'll go to the beach.)

You should attempt to answer the following questions (even just at a high level) toward the beginning of your conversation because your audience will be thinking about them subconsciously, hoping to hear the answers before they'll be open to the rest of the conversation.

- What is it?

    ○ This can also mean, *who are you, and why are you here?* Or something similar — if you're a stranger approaching someone, or if the topic is unknown.

- What's in it for me?

    ○ Once they understand why you're there, they need to see a connection between the value of what you're offering and the value to them if they buy the idea. At the very least, you want them to keep listening.

- What is the next step?

    ○ Often, people just need to listen, but sometimes there may be a call to action — if so, make sure you're clear what it is. What do you want them to do next?

    ○ Forgetting to let your audience know what to do next results in lost opportunities to help someone, and lost sales.

Example 1:

I want to sell more books (a sample conversation with a potential prospect).

What is it?

- My book is a collection of useful tools to help inspire people to action and success.

What's in it for me?

- Readers will find easy techniques to help them build their Confidence, have Clearer Direction in life, and improve their Communication skills.

What is the next step?

- There are three options if you want to learn these skills. Attend a training, order the book online, or download an electronic version for your Kindle.

Example 2:

Asking for a pay raise in a small company.

What is it?

- Hi, boss. I wanted to talk to you about a potential pay raise.

What's in it for me?

- I've been here for ten years and really know the system inside and out, so **you can rely on me**. I have been training all the new staff for three years, which **takes the workload off you and you don't need to hire anyone for that job.**

What is the next step?

- I was wondering if you'd be willing to **have a meeting** with me later this week **to discuss the possibility** of either more pay or some additional vacation days.

Maintaining a Conversation

The following sections cover a range of tools to help maintain the flow of the conversation and find out more about the person you are speaking to. You may have a question to ask, but if you don't feel the person is available for that question yet, use these tools to help create a stronger bond between you.

Meaningggg...

This word has an uncanny ability to help a conversation flow. It communicates that we haven't understood something and that we're gently asking for clarification.

If you ask a question and the person gives a short answer, use this method to keep the conversation flowing and find out more from them. Simply repeat a keyword from their response and add the word *meaning* with an extended *"g"* in response. For example:

How was your weekend?

Good.

Good meaningggg?

Well, I went to my friend's place to watch a movie on Saturday, and on Sunday I just chilled.

Chilled meaningggg?

Well, I grocery shopped in the morning and then stayed at home and made a roast dinner.

Out of context, this can sound strange, but I assure you that if you want someone to keep talking, they will do so if you use this word, as I have shown. Some people think that once you know this trick, perhaps it won't work on you...it does. In addition, I've found that I'm quite pleased if someone uses these techniques on me, as it suggests to me that communication is important to them and they want to hear what I have to say. Obviously, if you overuse the word, it will sound unusual, but I've personally never had that experience.

Pacing and Leading

When I studied to become a trainer of NLP in Australia, I learned about pacing and leading. This is a technique where you verbally align yourself with the other person and then guide where you want the conversation to go. It's far more effective than negating the person, which can turn the conversation into a battle or bring it to a close.

I see this as a verbal dance, and this led to my later studies in aikido, where the moves are designed to align and redirect the force. Unlike other martial arts, aikido does not focus on attack moves and primarily uses the energy of the attacker against themselves. Aligning and redirecting is another way of pacing and leading.

No BUTS. "Yes, and…"

To expand my speaking skills, boost my spontaneity, and enhance my confidence, I took an improv comedy course in Hollywood. We met weekly to practice our improvisation skills, and one of the key concepts was to use the phrase *"Yes, and…"* as opposed to *"Yes, but."*

The word *but* often has the effect of negating whatever was said previously. For example:

- I like you, *but*...

- You look good, *but*...

- You can eat it, *but*...

It doesn't even matter what they say next; we generally prepare ourselves for bad news.

It is helpful to minimize your unnecessary use of the word *but* and replace it where you can with the word *and*. This has the effect of aligning with the speaker and moving them to wherever you take them in the second half of the sentence. I am not suggesting that you never use the word, *but*. Simply keep in mind its effect of creating resistance and breaking down flow.

"Yes, and..." Conflict Easing and Flow Exercise

If you'd like to practice this skill in a safe confrontational situation to feel how it helps keep flow while avoiding conflict, find a friend and do the following:

Choose a topic (something in the news, a song you like, organic food, the climate, etc.) and make it into a two-sided argument: one of you argue for, the other against.

Each time either of you speaks, start your sentence with "*Yes, and*..."

Here's how a simple conflict example could go:

> *Tea is better than coffee.*
>
> Yes, and coffee has more caffeine in it, which is good because it keeps you alert.

Yes, and tea comes in a wide variety of flavors for everyone's taste.

Yes, and coffee has a rich, warming aroma.

Yes, and tea is easier to grow and cheaper to make.

Yes, and coffee...

Hopefully, you can see and feel the difference in the energy of the conversation and how it continues to flow when you adopt this phrase. (TIP: To feel the difference, say the same phrases, replacing the words *"Yes, and..."* with *"Yes, but..."*)

When you align with someone, they remain in a much more open state, so you are far more likely to achieve your outcome if, for example, you were asking for something. This is exactly the manner in which I would use this phrase if I wanted to park in a no-parking zone, and someone was preventing me. I would also keep in mind they would have those three primary questions in their mind: *What is it? What's in it for me? What is the next step?*

Sorry, you can't park there.

Yes, I understand, and we'll only be here for a moment to pick up a heavy package we bought at the store. (Notice I'm satisfying the question, "What is it?" in my answer as we discussed earlier because I know they're going to be wondering why we're stopping.)

But it's a no-parking zone.

Yes, I appreciate that, and we're not parking; we'll be moved in a few minutes, so I'm sure that will be okay, and we'd be really grateful to you. You'd be helping us out. If your boss comes, I'll tell them how helpful you've been. (Notice I'm answering the question, "What's in it for me?" We'll be grateful to them, they would be helping us, and we'll compliment them to their boss.)

No, you're not supposed to.

Yes, I see what you mean, and as I said, we'll be gone very shortly. Thank you so much for your understanding, and you're welcome to stay here to make sure we leave. (Notice here I'm directing him what to do and answering the question "What is the next step?")

Depending on the situation, I've found that staying committed to my required result three times is usually sufficient to get the outcome I want if it is possible. The rules by which you live are the rules that govern you but realize that you can have anything if you learn how to ask people appropriately and are willing to give them what they need.

I definitely don't use this strategy unnecessarily, but when I believe the outcome I want is genuinely for everyone's benefit or, at a minimum, is not going to put someone out too much or cause an issue, I will work toward it firmly yet flexibly.

If your ask is reasonable, I feel most people do want to help, so offer them a gentle opportunity to concede, and it can be a win/win situation.

I don't know... If you did know, what would you say?

Sometimes, when people are asked a question, they feel they will be committed to the answer, so are resistant to give a response and say that they don't know. If this happens, there is a useful phrase which can help: *if you did know, what would you say?*

This has the effect of giving people the freedom to provide an answer without feeling they are being committed to it and can change their minds. The fact is they already had that right (we always have that right); however, there is an illusion of more freedom here, which helps people feel at ease.

This question also has the effect of helping people see more resources if they do answer it. Sometimes, when answering one question, we realize how it affects something else, which may help us move forward or remove a roadblock.

When they respond, feel free to use meaningggg...to elicit more information from them.

What do you want instead?

Similar to the "if you did know" phrase, this question helps someone find more resources to help them overcome an issue. It also draws their attention toward a resolution to their predicament because if they identify clearly what they want, they can move toward achieving it.

Sometimes, when you ask this, you'll find that the person was just venting and wanting to be heard. They may realize this when you ask but, either way, this question has the effect of drawing what they say to a close.

In this example, Tony and Luke are friends, and some other friends, Helga and Sophie, are visiting from overseas. Assume Tony, the writer here, has been complaining for some time about not being invited out with their friends, and it's time to look for a solution.

> ...Luke even went to the show with Helga and Sophie and didn't ask me, despite them only being in town for four more days. They are always doing things

without me. I don't know why they don't tell me what they're doing.

What do you want instead?

I want them to tell me when they're going out so I can join them.

Great. You must let them know that because I think Luke is just wrapped up in entertaining them. Maybe you could text them now, so they know, and you don't miss out next time.

And, hopefully, from here, Tony would take some kind of action to resolve this situation if it was important to him, especially now that he knew clearly what he wanted. Using some of the other communication skills, Tony could ask to be involved either directly or in a message.

The following phrase is useful if someone keeps complaining about a topic, and you want them to move on.

So, what's the question?

This phrase has the effect of defining the problem so it can be resolved. When someone keeps complaining about something, but that thing isn't clearly defined, asking this question out of the blue can help nail down the problem. Inherent in asking the question is the assumption that there is a question to be asked, so people look for one, whether one exists or not.

In this example, a person is complaining about having to go somewhere because the last time they did, they had a bad time.

I don't understand why we have to go. Last time it was so hot, and the drive took so long, and when we got there, the room wasn't ready, and I needed a shower, and it meant that the whole trip was ruined. Remember how long it took to get service, too,…etc.

I understand. So, what's the question?

Ahem, well, can we stay at a different place this time, and can we stop on the way to break up the trip?

I'm sure we can find a way to make the trip more enjoyable. How about you look at the map and see where you'd like to stop, and I'll check our reservation.

I understand these are just fantasy examples, but I hope you can see the versatility of these phrases to help pace and lead someone by aligning and redirecting their attention. It may not solve the situation, but it will have the effect of moving things on. Now that you are aware of these tools, you'll be able to access them at the right time to help your conversations flow.

To continue with our example above, if the person responds that there isn't a question, try phrases such as the following to find out more:

- If there were a question, what would it be?

- I respect what you're saying, and what do you want instead?

4MAT[19] to Prepare You for Any Presentation

How would it feel to know you had a 4-step plan to deal with any presentation…ever! When you talk to people and are sharing information, there is a natural flow we tend to go through unconsciously to help make the presentation most

---

[19] *The 4MAT system was developed by Bernice McCarthy.*

effective. Some of us have a preference for one of the four steps; however, the beauty of the 4MAT method is that it addresses the learning/listening style of each type of person in relation to the speed at which they lose interest in the conversation. It is a fantastic training method which also explains the four primary learning styles. It is very helpful for creating engagement and ensuring you get results and can be applied to a range of areas, including presenting, sharing information, and writing blogs. The process is: **Why, What, How, What if?**

Feel

Questions	Discussion
WHAT IF?	**WHY?**

Do   *Watch*

HOW ?	**WHAT?**
Activity	Information

Think

Process:

Initially, it is important to **provide a brief overview statement** to contextualize the presentation. For example, if I were using this process to teach about the process itself, I'd start by saying: *the 4MAT process is a method for delivering information in a structured and easy-to-follow way that helps the audience and the speaker retain what has been said to get the most value.*

I'm briefly answering the question: **What am I delivering?** After a small amount of context, I'd go through the following steps.

1. **WHY?** Provide context to the conversation and start the discussion. What is the value of listening to you? Why are you telling me about this topic? Why should I listen to you? Why should I give you my time?

    a. This section is considered to be worth over one-third of the value of your communication, yet unfortunately, it is often completely overlooked.

    b. If people are WHY people, they may not switch on until this step has been fulfilled, so if you don't address those people first, they'll miss part of the conversation.

    c. There's no set time to spend here, but you should ensure that you feel you've fully answered the question of *why am I listening to you about this?*

        i. Example: *4MAT is worth learning because it is one of the best systems I've learned for sharing information, and I've studied adult learning for over twenty years. It addresses the primary learning and listening types. It is respectful to others. It provides structure to your delivery. It allows a natural flow. It helps you feel confident as you know the next step. It keeps you on track if someone asks a question ...*

2. **WHAT?** Provide the information about the topic. This is all about information and is the section most people spend ninety-five percent of their time in when delivering content. Data, quotes, handouts, information, and statistics are delivered here.

3. **HOW?** This is where you'd complete an exercise or interact with the audience if possible. This is HOW people really like to participate and get real-world experience. In a blog, this may be a question you ask at the end to encourage participation. HOW people want to understand how they can use the information or how it affects them. If you are a HOW person, this is the moment for you to reflect on how you'd deliver the first three steps of a topic you know.

4. **WHAT IF?** These are the question askers. They switch off the slowest and generally feel comfortable asking a question. They like to investigate the content in literal or hypothetical ways. You will see "WHAT IF" people show up in the comments section of a blog. They allow the audience to interact and for their questions to be asked. TIP: if you are delivering to a group, I recommend having a question or two up your sleeve to ask yourself as this often helps the audience

feel comfortable enough to ask a question. For example, "Many people ask: What would happen if I forgot a step?" and I would say, "Go back to that part and deliver it because you are the author of your own presentation."

You may not be delivering a full presentation, but being aware that this flow exists allows you to use it. Whether you are selling a product, writing a blog, giving a speech, or trying to borrow your parents' car, this flow can help dramatically.

Try 4MAT out today, and you'll see how easy it is.

Unconscious Tools of Persuasion

Robert Cialdini studied persuasion and psychology for years and identified six useful unconscious tools of persuasion in his book, *Influence, The Psychology of Persuasion*. The effects of these are touched on in some of the phrases already provided, however here are the six tools and how they can be used. These are invaluable for helping you guide a conversation because they usually result in a prescribed reaction from the person hearing them.

1. Try *Because* — It Works

If you use the word *because* when joining two related phrases, the person you are speaking to will often agree with the first phrase, simply because you said the second one.

I often use these phrases if I'm at a market trying to get a discount, and I'd say that once in three times, I get some kind of reduction or a free gift.

- Could I have a discount, *because* it's Wednesday?

- Is it buy five get one free *because* I asked for it?

158

- Will you take $10 for the lot *because* I only have big notes left?

The best way to learn this tool is to try it because that way, you'll see what happens.

2. The Law of Reciprocation

This law states that, due to our social conditioning, if someone does something for you, you will feel the need to do something in return. Notice how you feel if someone buys you a drink or pays for lunch — you naturally want to support them back — and because you know this, you can use this skill to your advantage. Just remember that if you offer something, you'd better be willing to follow through with it.

In addition, the law of reciprocation works, whether it was just an offer or if you do follow through with a gift or effort.

3. The Law of Contrast

This law is based on the fact that if an idea or thing has a certain frame of reference, then by changing the frame, the object is also perceived to change. Imagine looking at a mountain from the foot and from the top — they are two completely different experiences of the same thing.

The way to use this law is to start with a frame which is far more intense than the one to which you want them to agree — a course costing $850, for example. You must ensure that the customer believes you really want what you're asking for. Then change the frame of reference by reducing the price to a daily cost.

For example:

Can you afford a two-day course which costs $850? How about a course which costs $3 per day for a year? Which one is more expensive?

4. A Double Bind

This is an option that gives the other person the *illusion of choice*. "Would you like me to come around on Wednesday or Thursday? In the morning or the afternoon?"

This is a tool used by many salespeople, and you must be aware that if you hear this, you don't have to choose any of the options given. Recently, the concept of triple binds has surfaced:

Would you like that in red, blue or another color?

The key is to use the word OR in between the options and to stop speaking after you've given the choices.

5. Social Proof

When lots of people agree on a certain topic or follow a particular idea, other people are more likely to accept it. There is often a certain unspoken thought that *they can't all be wrong*. If many people are doing something, it appears to be more acceptable.

- Take a look at this book. Everyone is talking about it.

- We should go to the party; the whole group is going to be there.

- You should get an electric car. So many people have them.

Use social proof to help guide people to agreement in a conversation. Sometimes they may not be open to an idea yet, and social proof will help them remain open while you provide more information.

6. Commitment and Consistency

One of the strongest needs we have as a human is to stay consistent with our beliefs. As a result, if you get people to make small commitments consistently, they're like a train gathering speed. The more consistent they are, the less likely they will be to change their direction. This is called a *Yes Train*. Conversely, the fear is that if they become considered consistently inconsistent, society will often brand them as unreliable, which is not what they want.

In this example, assume that we are talking about a gym instructor trying to help a client remain committed:

> *It's so hard to get up early in the morning to train.*
>
> I agree, but you do want to look good this summer, don't you? (I deliberately used *but* because I wanted to negate what was said.)
>
> *Yes.*
>
> And you understand that to look good you're going to have to train?
>
> *Yes.*
>
> And, based on your target, you only have eight weeks to go.
>
> *Yes.*
>
> So, you can see that getting up early will help you achieve your target and is really a good thing in the long run? (This statement is arguably not 100 percent true, but because the client was on a Yes Train, they

would likely agree with it and be more committed to getting up early.)

Yes.

Please remember that you are encouraged to use these tools ethically and to help both you and others achieve more. If you try making people do things they don't want to, this is inappropriate and dishonorable.

Closing a Conversation

Depending on the context, a conversation may naturally close, or you may choose to close it. This is a very important skill to have because you may have some kind of call-to-action you want to share or a question you want to ask.

I talk to a lot of people at random in shops, events, and restaurants, and friends and family have told me they are impressed with my ability to approach almost anyone. I want you to have the same experience. That's why I'm sharing what I know. I have gone out on my own to parties, bars, or other venues from LA to Darwin to Hawaii, where I don't know anyone because I'm confident I'll meet someone fun to talk to and hang out with, or I'll just enjoy my own company. This isn't always the case, but more often than not, it is these days. For a lot of my career, I spent time on my own, so it was out of necessity that I improved these skills.

FYI, meet up groups and sites are also great resources to make new friends. They helped me a lot when I was in Australia and traveling around.

Don't Stay Past Your Welcome

I've heard that, after safety concerns, one of the biggest fears women have when approached by guys in a bar or at a party, is that the guy will stay there all night. I've checked with a number of women, and they agreed this was certainly a concern, which sometimes led them to be less friendly, even if they didn't mind the guy's company.

If you meet people when you're out, keep in mind they may already be in a group and have plans for their evening. Feel free to use your newfound confidence and communication skills to strike up a conversation and chat for a while; however, if you feel any kind of awkwardness after the initial connection, consider closing that conversation to explore other conversations. This does not mean you will not talk to them again; it just illustrates that you are an independent person. It also alleviates their fear that *you're* going to stay there all night. Later, you can swing by when it feels right to continue the connection.

Locking in an Appointment

If you want the person to agree on a time or date for further connection and you feel you need to be a bit more direct, you could use a double bind (*"So, would you like to meet this week, or next? The morning or afternoon? For a coffee or a juice?"*) Sometimes; it is nice to do this anyway, as most people prefer a small choice rather than unlimited options and remember, we can all always change our minds or choose an option that isn't offered.

"Every second is a second chance to make a new decision."

In keeping with the theme of meeting new people in a social environment, consider that if you are organizing catching up with someone, try not to choose the stereotypical options, unless you want stereotypical outcomes. A bar, restaurant, or perhaps seeing a movie are clichés when it comes to dating, so see if you can come up with other options. Also, keep in mind that meeting later in the evening can be a loaded option, so consider daytime events if you want to be less forward and get to know the other person better.

Ending a Conversation Comfortably

In the Interruption section below, I cover a few ways to break into a conversation if you're with a very talkative person (for example, by saying or asking their name). However, before we get to that, I will share with you how to end a conversation comfortably.

Kill the monster while it's small.

If you know you are going to be talking to someone who tends to talk a lot, let them know at the beginning of the conversation, how much time you have. You are welcome to extend past your own time limit, however as you have already mentioned it, it is far easier to remind the other person when you are ready to leave the conversation.

Around the beginning of a call, interrupt if necessary to say:

> *Hey Peter, just wanted to let you know that I have plans in about ten minutes so I can chat till then.*

Then after your 10+ have passed:

> *Peter, I don't mean to cut you, off but as I mentioned, I only had ten minutes. Let's chat again soon. It's been great hearing from you.*

The plans you have can be for anything, so if you need to book something on the fly, so you're not on the call in ten minutes, do it!

Why + Future + Goodbye

When you want to leave a conversation, use this simple recipe.

1. **Tell them Why you're leaving the call/conversation:** This could be for any reason, and it is important to remember that you don't owe anyone an explanation. You don't have to be rude, but if you simply say that you need to be somewhere else, then that's fine.

2. **Mention something about a future connection:** This creates a flow instead of stopping the energy because you are leaving. You could say, *"Let's catch up next week," "I'll call you,"* or *"I'll be in touch."* Anything like that will do.

3. **Say goodbye:** This clearly identifies you are leaving, so when you say it, it avoids the ambiguity of what's going to happen next. For example: *"Bye for now," "Thanks for the chat," "See ya."* Then hang up or leave the conversation.

Hopefully, these ideas will help you to deal with ending a conversation comfortably. Learn them and practice using them at different times.

Interrupting and Objections

These two behaviors strike fear into many; however, they are excellent opportunities if you know what you're doing. You don't need many ways to deal with conflict, as long as you find a method that works for you, and you may find this opportunity in interrupting or creating an objection.

Objections and Conflict

Contrary to what seems to be common sense, sometimes if you're selling someone an idea or product and they start objecting, this actually illustrates that they have some interest.

Objections are our way of saying:

"Some of what you're saying may work for me, but I have some issues, and here they are."

In this scenario, using a 100 percent objection, the response would be "No." So, if someone is objecting and willing to share their objections, they may be open to finding out a way to make the offer acceptable.

Often, we want to know more so we can determine our course of action. Meaning, if someone objects to you, you can use this as a signal that you need to do something different. You may need to reframe the situation, shed new light or, more importantly, get them to clarify the reasons they're objecting to see if you can overcome them.

I'm sure you have reasons for saying that. Do you mind if I ask what they are?

When someone disagrees with you, use the phrase:

"I'm sure you have reasons for saying that. Do you mind if I ask what they are?"

This helps uncover the underlying issue. Often, people don't state what's really going on, and this question does a great job of clarifying that. You can add on *is there anything else?* Or, use *Meaningggg...*if you want to go deeper.

Please note the word *good* is not found in this sentence. It is important to avoid saying:

"I'm sure you have *good* reasons for saying that..."

Adding the word *good* unconsciously justifies their answer and perspective, and if you contradict them, it will be harder to move them forward if you inferred they had *good* reasons.

How is that a problem for you?

Inherent in the word *why* is the feeling of justification. When asked why we do something, we usually respond by justifying our behavior. This can be helpful if that's the effect you want; however, if you want to find out somebody's reasons for doing something in a more neutral way, asking, *"How is that a problem for you?"* can achieve that.

Something to be aware of is that as a result of people preferring to avoid conflict, they will not tell you the most important reason first because they have a strong attachment to it and likely feel it is very challenging if they tell you directly. For this reason, it is respectful and also helpful to remember that many people have a three-time convincer strategy, which means that the third answer they give is likely the most important. So, when you get an answer to an objection after asking the question, *"How is that a problem you?"* follow it up a couple of times with:

"Is there anything else?"

Listen carefully to what they say and, before handling any objections, find out what is the most important reason (as mentioned, usually it's the third reason they give you).

The Agreement Frame: Agree/Appreciate/Respect and...

An outstanding skill to have in your toolbelt is the *Agreement Frame*. This is another clear method to align and redirect communication. It can be used to dissipate energy and guide the conversation with flow.

When we feel someone has empathy for, or agreement with, our perspective, we unconsciously feel our values are supported and tend to relax and feel more comfortable. This is what is achieved using the Agreement Frame.

Although hearing someone say, *I understand*, can be very powerful and help us feel connected to others, keep in mind that if someone is in a highly charged state, they can disagree with your assertion that you understand their position. This will block the flow of the conversation. The benefit of using the words of the agreement frame is that they are opinion-based words, which means they cannot easily be negated.

To use the frame, when someone says something you want to negate in any way, employ one of the following:

> I agree, and...
>
> I appreciate, and...
>
> I respect, and...

Taking the words, *appreciate* and *respect*, I hope you can see that you can always appreciate or respect someone else's view. When you do this, they feel heard and aligned with and will stay more open.

When I use the phrase *"I agree, and"* I consider I'm agreeing that *that is their perspective*, as opposed to agreeing with their perspective. It's a subtle difference, but it allows me to keep the integrity of what I'm saying and helps them feel respected.

A good way to practice using this tool is to follow a similar method to the "*Yes, and...*" exercise. Find a friend, choose a topic, and take sides on it, then discuss the topic using the *Agreement Frame* phrases.

Interrupting

Sometimes you will find yourself in situations where you can't break into the conversation because the other person or people are talking so much. At these times, it is valuable for you to know how to gracefully interrupt and then lead the conversation.

Get them to stop talking by saying their name.

If you're ever in a situation where you want someone to stop talking so you can speak, **say or ask their name.** Whether it's childhood conditioning or the importance we place on ourselves, hearing our name spoken catches our attention and stops us in our stride.

Once they've stopped talking, that is your opportunity to lead the conversation. There is a range of phrases and ideas I've covered that you can use to start the conversation afresh.

Nod your head three times to catch the attention of the speaker.

This is so strange, but the next time you're in a group of people and the speaker is not flowing you any attention, **nod your head at a medium pace three times** in response to something they say. Quite incredibly, I've found that, more often than not, they'll look at me. This is your opportunity to break into the conversation if that is your intention.

If you are interrupted:

In normal social environments, interruptions can form a natural part of the conversation. However, sometimes they hinder the connection or detract from what you are trying to deliver. The following suggestions are ways you can deal with being interrupted, but they are very much context-dependent, so learn them and then chose the tool you need at the right time.

If you are in the flow of telling a story or delivering information and you get interrupted *and don't want to be*, the first method to deal with that is to **ignore the interruption**. This may sound rude but, it is the reflection of the behavior they have demonstrated to you, and as somebody with important things to say, it is wise to remember that you don't have enough time to address every question people have for you. Consider what it's like talking to a child who keeps asking questions. When I've been delivering in a training environment to large groups, I have, at times, ignored repeated interruptions to ensure the flow of connection. Again, I'm not trying to be rude, but I'm calculating that the benefit from me continuing is greater than the loss of time or focus to deal with the interruption.

If you are using the 4MAT method to deliver your information, haven't covered the key points yet, or just want to guide your questioner, you can also let them know that you haven't covered all the information yet so could they save their question for the end? Then, when you get to the end, you can confirm whether their question has already been answered and if not, it's their chance to have it addressed.

Chapter 7:
How to Practice What You've Learned

We have covered a lot of material in this book, and it is possible you could be feeling a level of overwhelm. Here are a few ways to implement what you've learned, which I think are quite fun to help you enjoy the process.

Exercises with Friends

It could be fun to choose a phrase or idea from the book, discuss it, and then do the corresponding exercise. If there isn't one, make up an exercise and take turns trying each side — either for or against. If you're honest and playful, you can significantly help yourself, and a friend boost your confidence quickly.

Practice When It Doesn't Matter

When I play *Beat Saber VR* on my PlayStation, I feel like a master swordsman with my lightsabers as I slice with glowing swords the musical blocks flying toward me (Google the name, if you don't know this game). If I don't make a mistake for a while as I slice the notes, I become aware that I could get a perfect round, and I've noticed the moment I do that, I feel pressure. It doesn't take too long before I make a mistake. This doesn't happen every time, but I do feel the psychological pressure. Once I've made one mistake, I relax again and generally have a very good round because I feel the pressure has been released, and I have nothing to lose.

I'm telling you this story to remind you to practice some of the skills I've shared in situations where you don't feel pressure.

Similarly, when you compliment people you are not attracted to, you tend to feel less pressure to say the right thing, so when you want to compliment someone you do like, you'll already have confidence. Perhaps they have a nice smile or were extra helpful: there are always things to compliment in people if you look for them. As you interact throughout the day, give compliments out like they're free fruit.

Three-second Rule in Dating

If you are in the dating game and want to meet people when you're out and about, I recommend the three-second rule. It goes like this: if you see someone and like them, walk toward them to connect within three seconds. The first step is often the most difficult, yet it yields amazing returns. More people are unhappy today due to indecision rather than bad decisions, so simply take the first step and gather momentum. I share these tools because they work, and I remember that one of the two longest relationships I've had in my life came from the results of this exact tool!

Focus on Failure

You're good at getting it wrong, so why not use that as currency?

"If you focus on missing the target, you just might hit it!"

As humans, we subconsciously see there are infinitely more ways to do something wrong than to do it right. Take something as simple as setting a table with a knife and fork. There are a few ways to do it right, but if you turn either of the implements a few degrees, or move them anywhere else on the table, the setup is incorrect. I think it's time we gave failure some value because to fail, we have to take part.

A useful way to implement this technique centers around dating. Some single people complain about not meeting someone, but then literally never ask anyone out. They fear rejection of some sort, or perhaps they've never realized they could ask. Dating apps have made this process easier, but when it comes to meeting someone and starting a conversation, this skill (currently!) is all offline. So, I encourage people to aim for five rejections per week. You can count it how you like, but as you've probably realized, to get five rejections, you have to start the conversation at least five times! It's literally a win/win situation, and you can celebrate when you hit your target. Of course, if you end up missing your target because you're making new friends, well, that's perfect!

A good friend of mine once gave himself the task of speaking to 100 women to whom he was attracted within a week. It wasn't that he needed to ask them out on a date, but he needed to start the conversation to build his experience and skill. He said the first few were really hard, the next ten got easier, and by the time he was about halfway through, he was so much more confident and comfortable and was even having fun! In addition, he did end up having a few dates, and for a one-week commitment, that's a great result.

In this example, his score was kept by the number of attempts he made, irrelevant of outcome, so he had flipped the negative to help propel him forward when failure usually has the opposite effect.

The currency of success is failure, so when it happens to you, aim to see it as another piece of guidance from the universe instead of a criticism or that you've failed. If you can reframe the negative like this, it will give you even more flexibility and the ability to have a fantastic life.

Try one of my Inspiring Menus...

To make it easier for you, I have created a range of menus where you get to practice some of what I've shared in a structured way for a week. Turn the page and see what whets your appetite.

Inspiring Menus

In the past, I have been so frustrated when learning that at the end of the teaching, I became so overwhelmed that I didn't know where to start and didn't always take action.

As a result, I've developed a selection of menus to help you easily implement the ideas I have shared. They are made up as follows:

- Starter: Easy activity

- Main Course: Challenging or Time-Consuming activity

- Dessert: Something fun

Most of these ideas are designed to take place over a week; however, if you consider that your focus for that week is around that menu, then it can make practicing what you learn so much easier, better structured, and fun.

Keep a version of the menu handy and read it each day to keep the ideas in the front of your mind. By doing that, you'll unconsciously discover opportunities to practice, and in no time, your skills will be growing, you'll be getting more confident, clearer in your direction, and communicating more effectively.

As with a menu in a restaurant, you can swap between different menus to create à la carte menus based on what you're trying to achieve.

I have added a description at the top of each menu and have also included two menus that focus on Confidence, Clear Direction, and Communication.

Note about videos: I mention in some of the menus to watch a video on YouTube. Please check my website for resource links or go to YouTube.com, then search for *InspirationtoSuccess* to find my channel.

Determine Your Values Menu

If you haven't already, I strongly urge you to either go through my values section and do the exercise or go to drdemartini.com and follow the **Demartini Value Determination Process**.

Knowing and using your values can give you a real boost in the following exercises, and I recommend it as your first action.

Please schedule an hour one day to honor yourself and reveal what you've always known.

As this is such an important menu, once you've completed the exercise, you can take the rest of the day off. I give you my permission!

Build Confidence

This menu provides a taste of clothing changes to come while the main course uncovers the flavors that have created who you are. For Dessert, enjoy some wise and valuable tips from the TED stage.

Starter

- Fill a bag with at least five clothing items to give away or donate based on the tips in the External Confidence clothing basics section.
- Get a new piece of clothing in a more confident style, something which supports how you feel.

Main Course

- Go through the Un-conditioning Exercise.
- This will help you identify why you may have certain beliefs about your ability or what you can do.

Dessert

- Watch any TED talk about confidence.
- Search YouTube for *"TED Talk Confidence."*

Trust & Confidence, Success & Gratitude

This delightful option will fill you with gratitude as you finish the Starter. The Main Course (ideally served with the results from your Values Determination) helps create new possibilities, more aligned with who you are. The Dessert compliments this menu because you can do anything!

Starter

- Start your *Success and Gratitude List*. This can be recorded in a notebook or electronically but should be fun.
- Write something in it every day for a week.

Main Course

- Go through the Re-condition Yourself Exercise.
- This will help you clarify new beliefs that will support you and allow you to create the internal conditioning you need to achieve your goals.

Dessert

- Watch at least two videos in my YouTube playlist called *You Can Do Anything*.
- Search YouTube for "*InspirationToSuccess*" and navigate to the playlists.

Get Some Clear Direction

We start this menu with a simple consommé of a task, but don't let that fool you. What you may want may not be as clear as you think. This is followed by a hearty and satisfying planning session with another helping of inspiration from real people online.

Starter

- Write down five things you'd like to achieve with your career, relationships, or health in the next month.
- Chose things you have control over.

Main Course

- Take one or more of the items you noted previously and make a plan for it.
- Use the steps in the *How To Chunk It Down And Execute* section.
- Plan at least the first three steps and complete the first. Refine, add to and execute your plan for at 10 mins per day for a week.

Dessert

- Watch at least two videos in my YouTube playlist called *You Can Do Anything*.
- Search YouTube for *"InspirationToSuccess"* and navigate to the playlists.

Get Rewarded for What You Love

When you reflect on what you love, the main course will hopefully connect flavors and ideas in ways you haven't previously considered, which will lead to your reward. You know the drill; finish this menu with a taste of You Can Do Anything.

Starter

- Write down what you loved about the top 1-3 jobs you've had.
- Come up with at least ten things per job.

Main Course

- Go through the *How Can You Get Rewarded For What You Love To Do* exercise.
- This will help you create new connections so you can do more of what you love and be rewarded for it.

Dessert

- Watch at least two videos in my YouTube playlist called *You Can Do Anything.*
- Search YouTube for "*InspirationToSuccess*" and navigate to the playlists.

Quality Compliments Communication

This menu starts with a, "Wow, you have beautiful elbows," followed by a week of connecting with new people using simple ways. Your desert is a fun and interesting course which may take up more of your time than you think.

Starter

- Using the tools in the *Quality Compliments* section, compliment three people per day for a week.

Main Course

- Review the section on *Opening a Conversation* and use at least two of the key phrases over the coming week (e.g., Can I have your opinion?).
- Use the phrase at least twice per day over the coming week to talk to new people.

Dessert

- Watch at least two videos in my YouTube playlist called *Fun & Interesting stuff.*
- Search YouTube for "*InspirationToSuccess*" and navigate to the playlists.

Improve Your Communication and Influence

When we teach, we learn – start this menu with a tool which once learned, you'll have forever. I know you can't wait to get your teeth into the Unconscious Tools of Persuasion, so we'll end this menu with a flow exercise you can do with a friend.

Starter

- Review and teach someone the 4MAT method for delivering information.
- Ensure you draw out the four key segments or show an image of it.

Main Course

- Review the *Unconscious Tools of Persuasion* and practice using any of them at least once a day for a week.

Dessert

- Find a friend and practice the *"Yes, and…" Conflict Easing and Flow Exercise*.
- Then why not watch a video from one of my YouTube playlists – you pick!

Chapter 8: Conclusion

We've been on a voyage of discovery together, and you're nearing the end of this part of the journey.

What Have We Covered?

We started by looking at how things have changed in the world, which is now faster, cheaper, bigger, and offers more choice than ever before. Opportunities now exist in new occupations, including professional cuddler and specialist kidnapper; however, this is causing overwhelm in all our senses, and we're starving for direction. The new approach I have taught you revolves around having fewer choices and taking consistent steps in the same direction.

We looked at the 3Cs model and how it is an upward spiral to success.

Confidence has two sides. Internal Confidence: gives us a feeling of certainty on the inside and allows us to set goals and achieve them. External Confidence provides the fuel to reach out and connect with others.

Clear Direction is about identifying the next three steps at any time, so we can move forward confidently. We also learned that we don't need to know the destination to have a Clear Direction.

We looked at a range of phrases and tools to help with **Communication**. These create an atmosphere for connection and, when required, the stage to ask for what we need.

As we dove deeper into the model and Internal Confidence, we looked at how we may have kept some **conditioning** from our childhood or peers, which served us at the time it developed but is no longer helpful. In short, we learned we needed to evolve. We saw how our **comfort zones** are self-imposed limitations and that we are in control of challenging our boundaries and gaining new skills. We also reflected on our **self-belief** and how gratitude can strengthen it. I mentioned my Jedi mind-control tactics, thanks to my strong self-belief, which helped me get through passport control when leaving the UK for France.

In the External Confidence section, we looked at how our **appearance** and **attitude** play a large role in how others see us, and how we can improve these attributes through specific steps and actions. We covered how we can sharpen our game simply by brushing up on a few clothing basics or by spring cleaning our wardrobes. We remembered that we all have an incredible amount of knowledge in the things that are important to us, and everyone has a Ph.D. in Me! We spoke about rejection and how it provides us the feedback to achieve more success in the future as well as how it builds our confidence muscle when we gain experience. I did, however, remind you that too much of a good thing can be negative and how I nearly lost my right arm thanks to too much confidence.

When looking at Clear Direction, I encouraged you to know the next three steps (the micro-goals) in any moment that's important to you and to start dedicating time to completing tasks toward it. After building your muscle, you'll make longer-term goals over a week, a month, and then a year. You just need to know the next three steps. This simple method is used to help us manage so much complexity in life. Just knowing the next three steps at any time can give us peace.

In Communication, I stressed the importance of *asking effectively* and provided a range of phrases and sayings to help open people up to hear the message you want to share. I reminded you that if you don't ask, the answer is always no, and to look at how you can serve the people you're asking. We identified ways in which the tools can be practiced and noted that you'll get better at using these tools over time simply *because* you know they exist. We learned how to compliment effectively, that the top three questions in people's heads that we need to answer are: *What is it? What's in it for me?* And *What is the next step?* We learned that we should aim to answer those questions as early as possible to keep people open. We also explored how to interrupt people and deal with conflict by appreciating and respecting others, as well as aligning and redirecting them with verbal aikido.

Finally, we looked at ways you can practice the skills in this book and get yourself moving on an upward spiral to success using Inspiring Menus. These menus contain three courses of activities: The Starter is a simple task, the Main Course more challenging, and for Dessert, you are given a fun item to enjoy, which you can implement for a week.

Next Steps

Select one of the menus, grab your calendar, and schedule a week to practice the skills. Ideally, ask a friend, family member, or partner to join you in practicing the skills and, if you want to, make it into a game.

This Isn't Theory; This Is Practice

2014 was a very interesting year for me. I was at the end of my thirties; I had a job I enjoyed and was flying around Australia on a weekly basis, developing and delivering training in the mining industry. I worked long hours and made good money — but I spent a lot of time alone and would generally only be back in my home city of Brisbane for a week per month.

I wasn't in a relationship; the last one had ended about a year before. It was a messy ending, and, in hindsight, I can see that I stopped myself from looking for a relationship for about a year because of how I felt.

My **Internal Confidence** had been rocked, and my **self-belief** kept me from changing my situation. Then, one day in January 2014, I heard that my ex had met someone new, which triggered a change in me, alleviating the pressure I'd put on myself as a result of our relationship ending.

I took my own advice and focused on what the next three steps were to meet someone. I decided that to have a date, I should have tickets to a performance of some sort, so a few weeks ahead of a show, I bought a pair to the Chinese music and dance performance, *Shen Yun*. I didn't invite anyone.

I was only missing someone to go with, and, by chance, I thought of a friend of a friend I'd met a couple of times at parties but didn't know well. I used my **External Confidence** to reach out to see if she was interested in coming along. She was, and she did.

We were both very excited about being with each other, and before long, Joannah and I were going on adventures to rainforests and staying in the original Tropical Fruit World near Byron Bay. We took trips to the Hunter Valley wine area, as well as local excursions, and grew together in a very short time.

Being the overachiever I am, I somehow got it into my head that, seeing as everything was going well, we should move on to the next phase quickly. With my confidence glowing, I proposed to Joannah within a month of us being together. This may seem crazy to some, but in the back of my mind, I thought we should move along at a faster pace because, unfortunately, she had been fighting Hodgkin's lymphoma cancer for a number of years and although she was in remission, there was no saying what the future would hold. We planned to move to the Mount Warning area inland from Byron Bay and buy a café, where Joannah would paint, and I would teach and help run the place. I suggested we get married at Burning Man that August and started planning the event.

We lived in bliss for a couple of months before Joannah came to her senses and told me she didn't want to get married. I did not blame her for her decision and am grateful to her, as I think we moved far too quickly. Her wisdom prevented us from going down a very different path.

I offered her the tickets to Burning Man, but she refused them, so I ended up going alone.

When I lived in Emerald in Queensland, I used to go to the gem towns and markets of Sapphire and Rubyvale. There, I would buy buckets of dirt through which I would sift to find sapphires and natural zircons, as well as pick up some nice gems from local miners. During my time with Joannah, I took some of the stones I'd found and designed a two-banded wedding and engagement ring. Due to the timing, the ring arrived after we broke up, so I took it to Black Rock City (where Burning Man is held), which is also where I first met Erin. On the seventh day of the event, when the temple gets burned, and people often take the opportunity to let things go in life, I told Erin the story of my time with Joannah and gave her the ring as a gift. We had known each other seven days, and there were seven stones in the ring.

Little did I know the impact attending Burning Man alone would have on my life. After eight months of a long-distance relationship, I decided to finish my contract in Australia and move to Los Angeles to see if Erin and I would work together in a relationship.

Just over a year after moving my life to California, we were married! Erin and I now have a lovely house here and are continuing our life path together.

Sadly, I have to report that Joannah died in 2014, surrounded by her family, and in writing this piece, I've identified that it was exactly one year after I met Erin that she passed. I share this to remind you that no matter where you are now in life, a small change in your direction using even one tool in this book can lead to a completely different future.

You CAN Do It

Now it's time for action! No matter where you are, life can be completely different if you just take steps toward it and build your confidence for your own good and the people you care about. Expand your comfort zones, so you can handle more than ever before. Talk to more strangers and strengthen your resolve to give your gift by being the best you can be. In less than eighteen months, I went from being single and renting a shared flat in Brisbane to moving internationally for love, where we now own a home and love our lives.

Grab your calendar and schedule some time to practice your skills, build your confidence, and get clarity. Tell your friends about your newfound skills and, before you know it, your life will have changed forever.

"Every second is a second chance to make a new decision."

With love,
David

BONUS Material

I've added additional information here for those who would like some tips and guidance for building momentum on an upward spiral of success around physiology and language. This section will help keep your momentum going.

Physiology

Move with Confidence

- Minimize unconscious movements with your hands since this can make you look undirected.

- Minimize swaying and moving around unnecessarily. This is an unconscious safety mechanism many people employ when speaking in public; however, a grounded stance and moving with confidence conveys a much stronger message.

- Watch how people who are stereotypically confident move (these could be real people, or people acting in movies). Is there anything that you like about what you have observed? If so, adopt it for a few days and see how it feels. Perhaps it is something you find natural, too.

- If you feel stiff or just before doing something important, stretch your body in any way that feels comfortable. In nature, zebras do this when they're scanning for predators because it prepares their bodies and minds for action.

Stand Solidly (posture)

- Practice planting your feet when you talk to someone. You'll be surprised by how quickly people unconsciously notice and treat you differently.

- Keep your hands comfortably still. Don't be a statue, but avoid fidgeting too much.

Shoulders Back

- Slouching makes you look smaller and less than who you are. It's a good habit to hold your shoulders high, as it lifts your spirits and is healthier for your back and your general wellness. Imagine a thread from the top of your head, pulling you toward the sky as you sit or walk.

- Some tall people compensate for their height by bending a lot. When you don't need to do this, stand tall, as it's all-around better for you and your mental and physical health.

Eyes Up and Don't Be Shifty

- When walking, aim to keep your head and eyes up. This allows you to take in more of what's going on around you and is a more confident look. Some people find looking directly at others confrontational, so try these two handy tips:

  o If you're walking through a busy area, keep your eyes on a point just above everyone's heads in the direction you're heading. Depending on where you are, people will tend to move out of your way.

- As you walk down a street, comfortably look people in the eye and silently say to yourself, *I send you love*. This may sound corny, but it makes it very comfortable to look from person to person and not feel so awkward. Try it and see.

- When someone has shifty eyes, they are often considered dishonest; avoid moving your eyes all over the place. Aim to adopt a comfortable gaze with people without staring or looking away timidly. Remember to celebrate every victory as you maintain eye contact for longer than you have before.

Avoid Fidgeting

- In keeping with cleanliness and being tidy, ideally avoid nail or skin biting, as these can change how someone is perceived and how you see yourself.

- During conversation, when you touch your mouth, you are, in essence, hiding what you're saying, which is not a confident gesture. Avoid touching your face unnecessarily.

- Also, someone who is constantly on the phone does not emanate an air of confidence. This behavior gives the impression that they're not comfortable with where they are and that they long to escape.

Act Like You Own It

- Confident-looking people appear comfortable in many situations.

- This is not arrogance, but it's a sign they can deal with any issue that may arise. I think of James Bond and how he always seems calm and collected, despite impending doom.

Language

When speaking, we have many more tools at our disposal than just words. During confident speech, we'll use specific combinations of the following:

- **Pace or speed of speaking**
- **Tonality, timbre, pitch,** which all relate to the sound of the speech
- **Accent and eloquence,** which can subtly change how people perceive you
- **Words,** including the vocabulary we choose, and slang or sayings

Pace or Speed of Speaking

When we don't think we have anything of importance to say, we tend to speak more quickly.

- Avoid speeding up your speaking when you're nervous by remembering that what you have to say is important because you're saying it. Slow down and ease yourself into the conversation.

- If you tend to speak a lot or very quickly, aim to balance that out with slower, more deliberate conversation. If we think quickly, speaking more slowly gives us even longer to think about what we're saying.

- Practice pausing when you speak. It creates anticipation and gives you a chance to think more about what you're saying.

Tonality, Timbre, Pitch, Which All Relate to the Sound of the Speech

Deeper tones tend to be more commanding than higher pitched.

- Whether male or female, fill your lungs and speak with depth, as this will give you a more commanding presence.

- Some of us have telephone voices, which are different from our normal speech. Ask a friend to record you or record yourself on a call and see how you sound. I used to raise my pitch a lot on the phone, and now it's something to which I pay attention.

Accent and Eloquence Which Can Change in Certain Environments or with Different People

We all have accents when compared to other people, so appreciate the parts of your accent you like and play with them.

- Vowels tend to create rapport — notice the Romance languages (French, Italian, Spanish, Portuguese, and Romanian) are smooth, vowelly, and tend to sound appealing.

- In contrast, consonants tend to destroy rapport — think of German, Cantonese, and Russian. This speech is filled with consonants and can sound very harsh to the untrained ear, even when spoken lovingly.

- Aim to emphasize your vowels, and people will enjoy hearing you more. Practice reading poetry or short stories aloud, so you get used to hearing your own voice. *Aesop's Fables* are a quick and fun read if you ever want some short stories to practice on.

I consider eloquence to relate to the way we speak. Many people have told me they like my accent. For those who haven't heard me, it's naturally kind of a proper British accent with tastes of Australian and, some say, South African. It is quite soft and vowelly.

- Consider how clearly you pronounce your words when you're with new people or in situations where you would like to avoid being misunderstood.

- We get used to relying on phrases, sayings, and words that are common to where we spend our time. However, to people you meet from other environments (different countries, cities, towns, industries, work environments, scenes, etc.), it may be helpful to use more universal terms in order to be understood. When you're understood, you are more persuasive.

- Depending on the situation, you may also want to increase the amount of slang and local language you employ. When I worked in the mining industry in Australia, and we went on smoko (what Australians call a break), I'd chat with the guys and use much coarser language and swear more than usual. This helped me fit in and created better results for the training I delivered. It wasn't that I deliberately focused on doing this, but the environment supported that type of communication, and it was appropriate.

Words, Including the Vocabulary We Choose, and Slang or Sayings

Use your words effectively by selecting from the wide vocabulary you have.

- Words have a melody and can be enjoyable to hear, so using more multi-syllable words can give what you're saying some spice.

- If you don't know a word, look it up or ask the person who said it to explain it to you. Confident people are comfortable admitting to not knowing something and are willing to learn.

Transformational Vocabulary describes words that lead us to feel a certain way, such as bored, tired, fantastic, or amazing!

- Add some positively transformational vocabulary to your repertoire and aim to reduce some of the negative.

Side Story

I say the word "lucky!" a lot, and I definitely feel luckier. In an experiment I once saw, Derren Brown, a skilled British hypnotherapist and NLP expert, used suggestion and NLP in a small town in the UK to see if he could condition everyone to be luckier. The results of the experiment clearly identified that observation often determined luck. Unlucky people tend to be less observant than the lucky ones. So, perhaps add words and phrases such as "lucky!" and "I see" to your daily expressions.

Here are some examples of transformational vocabulary:

- "That's fantastic" vs. "good/okay."
- "I'm so excited to come" vs. "I suppose I'll come."
- "I get to do xyz" vs. "I have to do xyz."
- "I feel incredible," vs. "I'm fine."

Use a bit of variety with your words. A thesaurus will build your lexicon. When you are working in any range of programs on a PC, including Microsoft Word or PowerPoint, when your cursor is on any word, press **Shift+F7** on the keyboard to bring up the thesaurus. It's quick and easy to use.

And Finally, the Confidence Secret

"Good judgment comes from experience, and experience comes from bad judgment."
Rita Mae Brown

I think it's only fair to let you know that the confidence secret is also the elephant in the room:

Confidence comes from experience, and experience comes from doing things when you're not fully confident yet.

Now that you are at the end of the book head back to the Inspiring Menus and select some fun activities to practice for the week ahead so you can get on your upward spiral to success by boosting your Confidence, clarifying your Direction and improving your Communication!

Links to Exercises and References

Go to www.inspirationtosuccess.com to subscribe for free gifts, updates, the latest videos and upcoming workshop dates. You can also learn about coaching with me or choose one of my online courses or products.

Please also visit www.onemilliontouches.com and leave a comment which will help me reach my personal mission of impacting one million people in my lifetime.

About the Author

David grew up in Hong Kong, spent time on an island in Scotland, and then lived north of London for fifteen years. Travel has been his way of life, and he has been to and worked in locations such as France, New Zealand, Australia, USA, and the UK. His extensive personal studies and life experience in over thirty countries have led him to uncover fundamental skills and tools in confidence, purpose, and communication, which have provided him with incredible opportunities and living wealth.

During his earlier career, he worked for organizations such as Accenture, Coca Cola, and Barclays Bank until he realized that kind of work didn't satisfy his desire to connect and contribute. He decided to move to New Zealand and then Australia for two and a half years on a Kombi excursion to have fun and find himself. This provided the adventures and debt you can probably imagine. He returned to the UK inspired by some learnings from Tony Robbins, although he was not clear on his next step.

At this point, life wasn't all roses so two years later, and after listening to a motivational CD one cold, miserable evening in a leaky rainy flat in Manchester, he made a decision to move to Australia on a whim and a prayer. He was $65,000 in debt with no job or visa to work, no family around him, and almost no friends, but still, he moved to Australia. Incidentally, he had never been to Brisbane before, and he chose it because it was the biggest city, in his favorite climate, in his favorite country.

Over the following years, he paid off nearly $100,000 in debt and worked on billion-dollar projects for international organizations in their project and training departments such as Rio Tinto, Boeing, BHP Billiton, Queensland Government, and Los Angeles Children's Hospital and City of Hope Research Hospital.

He is certified as a Demartini Values Facilitator and also trained in the Demartini Method. He is a Master Coach and has completed Neuro-linguistic Programming training to the Trainer's level as well as he is a certified hypnotherapist. In addition, David has created materials for international personal development speakers as well as his own books, materials, and courses.

His purpose is to help inspire people to fulfill their purposes. He achieves this through teaching and sharing core knowledge about Confidence, Clear Direction and Communication using practical technology, and the written and spoken word as well as experiential activities.

David also created www.onemilliontouches.com as part of a mission to impact 1,000,000 people in his lifetime. Head over and leave a note if you've been impacted by him. It would be appreciated.

> *"Unconventional Creativity is the*
> *secret sauce I like to add to life."*
> David Alan Woodier

www.inspirationtosuccess.com

info@inspirationtosuccess.com
Los Angeles, California

Disclaimer

Although the publisher and the author have made every effort to ensure that the information in this book was correct at press time and while this publication is designed to provide accurate information in regard to the subject matter covered, the publisher and the author assume no responsibility for errors, inaccuracies, omissions, or any other inconsistencies herein and hereby disclaim any liability to any party for any loss, damage, or disruption caused by errors or omissions, whether such errors or omissions result from negligence, accident, or any other cause.

This publication is meant as a source of valuable information for the reader; however, the publisher and author assume no responsibility for any actions or inactions taken as a result of this book. It is not meant as a substitute for direct expert assistance. If such level of assistance is required, the services of a competent professional should be sought.

Made in the USA
San Bernardino, CA
10 August 2020

76754865R00124